The A-Z of curiosities of the
YORKSHIRE DALES

© Summer Strevens, 2015

All Rights Reserved. No part of this publication may be reproduced, stored in a retrieval system, or transmitted in any form or by any means – electronic, mechanical, photocopying, recording, or otherwise – without prior written permission from the publisher or a licence permitting restricted copying issued by the Copyright Licensing Agency, 90 Tottenham Court Road, London W1P 0LA. This book may not be lent, resold, hired out or otherwise disposed of by trade in any form of binding or cover other than that in which it is published, without the prior consent of the publisher.

Moral Rights: The Author has asserted her moral right to be identified as the Author of this Work.

Published by Sigma Leisure – an imprint of Sigma Press, Stobart House, Pontyclerc, Penybanc Road, Ammanford, Carmarthenshire SA18 3HP.

British Library Cataloguing in Publication Data
A CIP record for this book is available from the British Library.

ISBN: 978-1-91075-809-0

Typesetting and Design by: Sigma Press, Ammanford, Carmarthenshire

Cover photographs: *top (left to right)*: memorial to Adam Sedgwick, Dent © Summer Strevens; The Cow and Calf Rocks, Ilkley Moor (courtesy of Snapshots Of The Past); The Druid's Temple, Swinton Park Estate © Summer Strevens; Bedale Leech House © Summer Strevens; *main picture*: Marmion Tower, West Tanfield © Summer Strevens

Photographs: © Summer Strevens, unless stated otherwise

Printed by: Akcent Media Ltd

Disclaimer: the information in this book is given in good faith and is believed to be correct at the time of publication. No responsibility is accepted by either the author or publisher for errors or omissions.

The A-Z of curiosities of the
YORKSHIRE DALES

Summer Strevens

Acknowledgments

The compiling and writing of this book has been a fascinating and absorbing experience, and in spite of my own personal enjoyment in the name of research, I would like to express my gratitude to a number of people without whose help and support, especially in the acquisitions of images, this publication would have been much diminished.

Grateful thanks are due to Miss Tor Jones, who proved herself chauffeur extraordinaire, regardless of my parlous map reading skills, and to Mrs Heather Jones (no relation) who both showed a tirelessly energy and verve in my quests for photogenic shots of the many Curiosities featured on the following pages – literally keeping up with the Joneses!

Special commendation is also due to my long-suffering partner, Jack Gritton, without whose technical assistance and enduring patience and support I would have been lost.

Many churches were entered on my quest, and grateful mention should be made of Gail Squires, Cathedral Secretary at Ripon, of Heather Lovett, Verger of St Anne's, Catterick Village and thanks to Kathy Couchman, Rector of St Alkelda's, Middleham.

I am also indebted to Margaret Halliwell for access to some of her antique and fascinating texts, and also to the endless list of those generous souls of the Yorkshire Dales who have shared of their time, experiences and memories with unreserved enthusiasm; their knowledge and the Yorkshire penchant for an enduring collective folk memory have proved invaluable in exploring the weaves that make up the very colourful fabric of the Dales.

To all those mentioned above, and everyone else who has given of their time, guided, advised and inspired, Thank You.

Summer Strevens
2015

Introduction

I am fortunate enough to have been living in the Yorkshire Dales now for over half a decade; a meagre tenancy I know in the scheme of the generational residency of some of my neighbours, I am certainly still regarded as something of an 'offcumden' – a Dales word used to describe people 'not from round here'! Nonetheless, while living here I have been able to indulge, unbridled, my inveterate habit of collecting all kinds of oddities and out-of-the-way information; the Dales occupy a region that produces much originality and the Yorkshire folk's pride in their individuality means that where that originality has been carried to a wonderful excess, eccentricity blossoms.

Set in some of England's most impressive and unspoilt scenery, the Dales are also a fertile breeding ground for the many and varied tales and legends concerning the numerous oddities scattered throughout the landscape, where the wind bends even the stubborn heather. Evolved from the underlying bedrock created more than 300 million years ago into panoramas of unquestionable character and charm, as well as the many geological curiosities crafted by Mother Nature, the region also boasts a proliferation of idiosyncratic man-made edifices, not to mention some odd noteworthy personalities and equally baffling traditions.

Strongly regional in feeling and form, while collectively the Dales are distinctive in their continuing life and their incomparable scenery, diverse as they are, each Dale has its own characteristic features, folklore and legends... Dialects linger and distinguish dale from dale. And life is deeply seated here. Bygone practices and customs are not forgotten, be it in the old methods of haymaking and sheep clipping or the traditional fairs and sports of the past still enjoyed, competitions of quoits are still commonplace. And while in times past, few Dales folk ventured from one dale to the next, self contained and separated from their neighbour by inhospitable countryside, now they are accessible to the world.

In compiling this collection of often peculiar riches, rather than use the tried (or *tired*) and tested method of plotting each curiosity by location, I have opted to alphabetise the treasures found within the 'classical' definition of the Dales region, encompassing the Yorkshire Dales National Park and the Nidderdale and North Pennine Areas of Outstanding Beauty. While some of the towns and villages mentioned are on the fringes of these boundaries, and where I may have wandered off my title page, I hope the reader will forgive me if I have strayed slightly to include the odd tale or feature from a location not strictly adhering to these borders, as in these cases exclusion on a point of strict geographical stricture would rob the following pages of some of those wonderful curiosities worthy of inclusion with the others. Where mention of one curiosity is pertinent to another I have referenced the associated entry by the letter it falls under, and if you wish to visit any of the Curiosities their locations are noted to the nearest town or village in the header – for those occurring 'county wide' the various locations are referenced in their description.

Discovering and compiling over two hundred Curiosities from around the Yorkshire Dales has been a pure joy for me; as well as some good old fashioned hard historical research, I had the glorious opportunity of tapping into the many rich veins of anecdote and folklore concerning people and places, strange edifices, unusual monuments and natural wonders. Whether you live in the Dales, are a visitor to the area or just plain interested in the Curious, I hope you will enjoy this book as much as I have enjoyed researching and writing it.

Summer Strevens
2015

A

AA Box, Aysgarth

An unusual sight greets the driver on the south side of the A684, just over a mile before the turn to Aysgarth Falls travelling 'up dale' from West Witton – an original timber AA telephone box of a type dating to around 1956. This bright yellow and glossy black rectangular kiosk numbered Box 442 is liveried with AA plaques on the gable of each side.

Once a common sight on the UK's major roads, with a network of over 1,000 boxes at one time, the Aysgarth box along with just a handful of other survivors has been listed in order to preserve this motoring curiosity.

The Aysgarth AA Box

Agra Moor Standing Stone, Costerdale

In the little known and beautiful vale of Costerdale, landscaped with high moorlands patterned with drystone walls, if one follows the swerving uphill path to the top of Slipstone Crags, a glance across the small valley will reveal the lone Agra Standing Stone. Protruding from the heather some four and a half feet tall the Agra Stone shares the moor with two close neighbours, though now virtually peat covered these companion stones may once have stood upright before falling and sinking into the ground. Located on flat moorland overlooking the confluence of Brown Beck and Birk Gill, these stones were clearly sited at a point of ritual significance to those Neolithic engineers for whom the sacred nature and importance of such locations is mirrored by the number of other distinctive British Neolithic ritual monuments marked by their proximity to water.

A little over half a mile to the south-west are the West Agra Cup and Ring Stones. A set of carvings covering about ten rocks, while most exhibit typical cup and ring designs no more than a few centimetres across and consisting of a concave depression pecked into the rock surface and surrounded by concentric circles, one of the boulders at West Agra displays a curious form of megalithic art with some unusual carved motifs accompanying the depiction of what appears to be a stylised man.

Ais Gill Summit, Mallerstang

Dominated by the mountainous bulk of Wild Boar Fell, the Settle-Carlsile Railway Line reaches the highest point of any mainline railway in England at Ais Gill Summit, some 356 meters (or 1,168 feet in old money) above sea level, carried over the Ais Gill beck by a small viaduct. There have been three notable rail accidents nearby, tingeing the line with tragedy, the most serious of which occurred on Christmas Eve 1910 with the incident known as the 'Hawes Junction' rail crash that claimed 12 lives.

The crash occurred when a busy signalman forgot that a pair of light engines were waiting on the northbound side of the line bound for Carlisle, and on clearing the signal for the approaching high speed Scotch Express travelling from St Pancras to Glasgow, the express and light engines collided just after the Moorcock Tunnel near Ais Gill summit. Almost entirely derailing the express train with disastrous consequences, casualty numbers were exacerbated as the timber-bodied coaches over-rode each other and then fire broke out, fuelled by the leaking gas feed for the coaches' lighting and ignited by the coals from the steam locomotives' fireboxes. The bodies of the unfortunate 12 victims (some were trapped in the wreckage and horrifically burned to death) were moved to the cellar of the nearby Moorcock Inn which served as a temporary mortuary, the dead subsequently buried at St Margaret's in Hawes where their memorial can still be seen in the churchyard.

Aldborough's Amphitheatre

In the summer of 2011 the discovery on the summit of Studforth Hill, just outside the village of Aldborough near Boroughbridge, ended centuries of speculation as to where, or indeed whether, the lost oval amphitheatre of Aldborough existed. Beneath the turf today grazed by cattle, geomagnetic sensors identified a curving bank of tiered seats that were part of what was once the largest outdoor arena in northern England. The team of researchers from Cambridge University were assisted in their search by a local woman whose grandfather had told stories of a legendary Roman amphitheatre beneath the hill she used to sledge down when she was a little girl.

Though most of the amphitheatre's seats were destroyed centuries ago, beneath the top of Studforth Hill the surviving spectator section has remained a secret for centuries, with archaeologists believing the amphitheatre to have been adjacent to a Roman sports stadium. The latest in a long list of Roman archaeological discoveries made around Aldborough, the discovery of the amphitheatre has added to the growing consensus that the northern province known as Britannia Inferior was centered on Aldrorough, or Isurium Brigantum to give the village its Roman name, with a greater and more prosperous and cultured population than previously thought.

Alkelda – Saxon Saint strangled with her own plaits!

There are in fact only two churches in the UK dedicated to this unusual Saint and both are to be found in the Yorkshire Dales, at Middleham and Giggleswick. According to legend Alkelda was a Saxon Princess who was murdered by two Danish women for her Christian beliefs in 800 AD, a time when the Norsemen were ravaging the ancient kingdom of Deira, the then Anglo Saxon territory into which Middleham once fell.

By tradition St Alkelda met a violent end by strangulation, either with a napkin or her own long hair – whatever the *modus operandi* of the wicked Viking womenfolk, the moment of her death is depicted in stained glass in Middleham Church. Saint Alkelda may also have been buried at Middleham, as here in the nineteenth century during restoration work a very primitive stone coffin was discovered under the floor, near the spot where, according to tradition, St Alkelda was interred. The coffin contained some human remains, which were declared by the experts to belong to a female. Bones were reburied close to where they were found and a brass plaque near the most easterly pillar on the south side of the nave marks the spot.

Stained glass in St Alkelda's Church, Middleham, showing the moment of the saint's martyrdom

Middleham has one further claim on the strangulated saint as close to the church is St Alkelda's Well, a sacred spring once venerated as a holy well, and said to be particularly efficacious in curing eye complaints.

In common with Middleham, as well as the church sharing the saint's dedication, at Giggleswick there is also a renowned ancient well, known as the 'Ebbing and Flowing Well' – for more about these mysterious 'breathing' waters see the well's entry inder the letter 'E'.

Almscliffe Crag, near North Rigton

Overlooking the road between Harrogate and Otley, Almscliffe Crag is hard to miss as this outstanding Millstone Grit outcrop is visible for miles around in just about every direction. Known as one of the best climbing locations in the district, with such classic challenges as the 'Parsons' Chimney', the 'Black Wall Eliminate', and the 'Wall of Horrors', Almscliffe Crag is also decorated with a form of prehistoric art; there are a number of cup marks carved on top of the crag as well as a large bowl shaped depression atop the outcrop known locally as the 'Wart Well' as supposedly the rainwater collected therein is imbued with the power to cure warts!

There is also a creation myth attached to the Crags, of the great giant Rombald who lived on Ilkley Moor long, long ago. Having gotten himself mixed up in an argument with the Devil, Almscliffe Crags were purportedly the result of the dark one's poorly aimed missile, missing Rombald and falling just short

The Millstone Grit outcrop of Almscliffe Crag dominates the skyline for miles around

of North Rigton Village. (The Devil seems to have been a perennially bad-shot – see the letter 'D' and the 'Devil's Arrows' for another of his missed targets).

A whiff of Faerie folklore also lingers about Almscliffe; the 'Faerie's Parlour' on the northwest side is supposedly the entrance to a small cave believed to lead to the supernatural realm of the Little Folk. Many people have scrambled down into the cave but have found no evidence of an elfin ingress point, though William Grainge writing in 1871 recounted how the fairies here "*were all powerful on this hill and exchanged their imps for children of the farmers round about*". It has to be said that the surrounding area is also imbued with an excess of faerie folklore, but an equally incredible tale tells of a live experiment where a goose was once pushed through the opening of the Faerie's Parlour only to emerged some considerable time later from a well near Harewood Bridge – 3½ miles away!

Angel Lectern, Thornton Watlass

The villages of Thornton and Watlass were still listed as two separate settlements at the time of their mention in Domesday Book in 1086, harking back to an era when the now fragmented pieces of Anglo Saxon cross head incorporated into the stonework of St Mary's porch would have been whole. The original nave and chancel of the Norman stone church built in the eleventh century are now entirely masked by the perpendicular rebuild of 1868, however some past features of note remain, namely the sturdy fortified tower built in early fourteenth century. Probably used as a watch tower forewarning of the prevalent threat of Scottish raiders, from the top on a clear day thirty other churches can be seen including York Minster. The tower may also have served as a place of refuge in times of strife as about half way up a door opens onto a small windowed room with a fireplace and a lavatory.

Turning to our alphabetical curiosity, St Mary's boasts the superbly carved Angel Lectern. Once

The Angel Lecturn, St Mary's Church, Thornton Watlass

the figurehead of a ship, claimed from an old sailing vessel discovered over 100 years ago in a Hull marine store by the then lord of the manor Sir Charles Dodsworth, the Angel was adapted by a local carpenter. The unexpected appearance of this lectern has been known to give more than one visitor a mild start, a departure from the usual eagles and pelicans upon which bibles are perched, perhaps the darkened wood lends this angel his somewhat sinister cast. Behind the Angel Lectern is the memorial chapel of the Dodsworths of Thornton Hall, owners of the manor since 1415; Sir Charles lies in the family vault beneath the north transept, not so far from his strange, dark acquisition.

Arthur's Oven, Hudswell, near Richmond

High above the south bank of the River Swale the ancient village of Hudswell, mentioned in Domesday Book, lies just upstream from Round Howe, a tree covered rock mound close to which is a large natural cave known as Arthur's Oven. Best access is from the village down a flight of 365 steps leading down to a riverside walk through pleasant woodland. The obvious fissure in the limestone supposedly connects via a secret tunnel to a subterranean cavern beneath Richmond Castle, about a mile away as the crow flies, where legend has it that King Arthur and his Knights lie sleeping.

The Arthurian association with Richmond Castle is borne of the old local myth concerning Peter Thompson, a local potter who found his way in (or was shown by a mysterious stranger in some retellings) to a cavern below the castle via a secret tunnel where King Arthur and his knights slept, ready to be awakened in time of national need. Thompson came upon Arthur's sword and horn lying on the ground next to the slumbering warriors, and though frightened, curiosity drove the potter to partially draw the blade from its dusty scabbard, but in so doing the knights began to stir – terrified he replaced the sword and understandably forewent blowing the horn, making a dash for the entrance. As he fled a voice boomed behind him "*Potter Thompson, Potter Thompson, if thoust had drawn the sword or blown the horn, thou hadst been the luckiest man e'er born*". The terrified Thompson supposedly blocked the entrance hole and it remains hidden to this day...

Aysgarth's Edwardian Rock Garden

The Aysgarth Edwardian Rock Garden, an accessible gem open to the public, was commissioned by Frank Sayer-Graham (1859-1946) in 1906 when the vogue for rock gardening was undergoing something of a popular revival. Sayer-Graham was a local landowner who also traded in silver rabbit fur, farmed from the purpose built warren in the lee of the hauntingly lovely Lady

Hill to the west of Aysgarth village (see the letter 'L' for more of Lady Hill's legends and mysterious association with the Faeries). Sayer-Graham is said to have held the distinction of supplying the last Czar of Russia with a silver fur stole.

With his first wife Mary, Sayer-Graham modernised Heather Cottage, his childhood home opposite the Rock Garden, into the model of Edwardian modernity, an embrasure of the Arts & Crafts movement so favoured at the time. Complementing the house the Rock Garden, complete with mountain stream and pool took the best part of eight years to construct, with each rock being brought some three miles from Stephen's Moor at Thornton Rust on a low horse-drawn cart. Planted with alpines specimens that flourished in the Dales climate, in Sayer-Graham's lifetime the garden was very much a private space, Mrs Sayer-Graham often rapping on the windows of Heather Cottage if any child dared so much as to touch the railings.

Following Sayer-Graham's death the Rock Garden passed through several hands, and in 1988 was saved from development when English Heritage stepped in with an emergency Grade II listing.

Today, thanks to accommodating owners and financial assistance from the Yorkshire Dales Millennium Trust, extensive restoration and replanting has ensured that Aysgarth Edwardian Rock Garden is preserved for generations to come – and admission is free!

Aysgarth's Edwardian Rock Garden

B

Barden Triangle, Wharfedale

Perhaps not in the same league as its Bermuda namesake, the Barden Triangle is however imbued with a definite measure of the mysterious. An expanse of supposed supernatural activity encompassing the villages of Appletreewick, Burnsall, Linton and Grassington, each village in turn claiming varying haunting manifestations of their own. Also within the boundaries of the triangle is the haunted limestone gorge of Troller's Gill (see the letter 'T' for further details of this malevolent location) as well as Elbolton Hill – 'Hill of the Fairies' – one of the strangely shaped Cracoe Reef Knolls inhabited by the Little Folk and said to possess magical properties. Also falling within this mysterious wedge of Lower Wharfedale is Dibble's Bridge, supposedly built by the Devil in a moment of rare generosity for a local shoemaker who shared his drink with him. And nearby Dibb Gill is also associated with the exorcism of another nasty, noisy ghost, Thomas Preston, one time seventeenth century owner of Low Hall in Appletreewick and some time terrorizer of Lower Wharfedale with his bangs, groans and yells from beyond the grave. The spur for his hauntings dating back to the mid-eighteenth century are unknown, but the disturbances were percussive enough to unseat ornaments from local mantelpieces! A priest finally laid the spirit in the Gill, hence the area is now known as Preston's Well.

Barden lays further claim to ghostly fame in the reports of chilling screams coming from Barden Tower, the ruined former fortified hunting lodge on the edge of the road leading up Lower Wharfedale between Bolton Abbey and Burnsall. Before the tower fell into a ruinous state after the lead and timbers were robbed from the building in the 1780s, a high pitched echoing scream was often heard from within the walls, and while these cries terrified visitors,

The ruins of Barden Tower

the locals simply tolerated the unearthly sounds with unflinching acceptance as merely a 'shout from hell'.

Barefoot Street, Ripon

So called as this was the route taken by pilgrims en route to St Wilfrid's shrine in Ripon Cathedral, in the middle ages it was common for pilgrims to walk barefoot as a visible sign of their humility and penance for their sins.

One of the oldest places of Christian worship in Europe, Ripon Cathedral was founded by Wilfrid in 672 AD, and his shrine brought many pilgrims to the city. Though the Saxon crypt is the only survivor of Wilfrid's original church, visitors can still go down into the underground chambers, virtually unchanged from the time when pilgrims would have come to venerate relics brought back from Rome by the cathedral's founder in the seventh century.

Battle Cross, Aldborough, near Boroughbridge

Removed from it's original position in neighbouring Boroughbridge in 1852, today this commemorative stone pillar, replete with informative blue plaque, stands close to St Andrew's Church where the Aldborough Road splits into Low Road and Chapel Hill.

The 'Battle Cross' is monument to the Battle of Boroughbridge, fought on 16th March 1322 between Edward II's army and the rebel forces under the command of the Earl of Lancaster. This bloody engagement fought for strategic control of a narrow

The Battle Cross, monument to the Battle of Boroughbridge fought in 1322

bridge and a nearby ford where the Great North Road crossed the River Ure resulted in the utter defeat of the rebels, and Humphrey de Bohun fighting on the losing side met a particularly gruesome end, fatally speared from beneath through a hole in the bridge timbers! Today a sturdier stone bridge spans the Ure, bearing a stone plaque stating that the downstream side dates from 1562 and the upstream (after further widening) from 1784. As for the site of the battle, while in 1322 Boroughbridge probably didn't even extended as far as the bridge that gave the town it's name, the bloody field has not entirely been engulfed by urban expansion and public access along the river banks allows easy appreciation of the key areas of the engagement.

Bee Boles

Bees were an once an essential element of the rural economy, both for the production of honey (when sugar was still an expensive imported luxury) and for pollinating fruit trees; consequently 'Bee Boles' were often built into the walls of kitchen gardens to hold hives. Designed to house the round wicker hives known as *skeps* which were commonly used in Britain from the twelfth century up to the mid-1800s, these were mostly replaced by the wooden bee hives still used today, hence the few remaining examples of Bee Boles still in existence. Sometimes the skeps were just placed on a bench or a ledge, but where weather conditions (such as those prevalent in North Yorkshire!) were not always ideal, these special shelters were built to protect the hives. There are still a few excellent examples of Bee Boles in the Dales, namely those set into the wall of Higher House in the village of Hebden near Grassington, and at 'Taitlands' near Stainforth, a small mansion house built in the 1830s. Further fine Bee Boles can be found in the remains of the walled kitchen garden of the seventeenth century Nutwith Cote Farm near the charming market town of Masham, and here the Bee Boles are conveniently situated next to what was once the orchard, the sole survivor of which is an ancient pear tree.

Beeswing Inn, East Cowton

Unrelated to Bee Boles, the Beeswing is a public house in East Cowton, near Northallerton, and is so named for a champion thoroughbred racehorse hailing from the north of England. Beeswing (1833-1854) was renowned as the greatest racing mare in Britain, in fact one of the greatest racehorses of all time... She was run on many courses between 1835 and 1842 and proved a real crowd pleaser. Entered into 63 races, she won an incredible 51 times, and of the 57 races that she finished, she was placed no lower than second on only one occasion. Beeswing's most notable victory was the 1842 Ascot

Gold Cup, but she also won the Newcastle Cup an incredible six times. After winning the Doncaster Cup for the fourth time Beeswing was put out to a well earned retirement. Many of today's top racehorses can trace their pedigree back to Beeswing and I dare say that a fair few of the pints pulled at the Beeswing Inn are supped in celebration of the winning racing progeny of the pub's namesake.

Beware of the Barguests!

While tales of spectral black dogs are legion throughout the British Isles these creatures are certainly no stranger to the Dales, and while they are known by different names in different parts of the country – in Norfolk they are Shucks, Gallytrots in Suffolk, while the Trash marauds Lancashire and Padfoots are seen in Staffordshire and Wakefield – our Yorkshire dark hounds are commonly termed as 'Barghests'. And the most famous of the Dales pack of hell hounds must be the 'Headless Hound of Ivelet Bridge'. The Headless Hound's manifestation is regarded locally as a seriously bad omen, and as Ivelet Bridge is located on the 'Corpse Way' this belief may well have been encouraged in the past by the stories of burial parties seeing the dog run on to the bridge only to disappear over the edge, understandably lending more weight to the ill fortune theme – for more of the aptly named Corpse Way and associated Coffin Stone see the entry under the letter 'C'.

Another, yet unusual variation on the demonic dog theme is the rainbow eyed Barguest seen about the village of Grassington. Known as the 'capital of Upper Wharfedale', the tally of visitors to one of the National Park's premier hotspots seem unaffected by this resident beast, said to announce itself with a rattling noise before materialising.

There are even accounts of multiple 'black dog' sightings in the Dales, one such made by a cyclist returning from an evening church service in Swaledale back in the 1930s. Having reached Barton Quarry just after midnight he saw a 'large dog-like figure' with flashing eyes and foaming tongue emerge on to the road. This first dog was grey in colour but unexpectedly followed at five yard intervals by a succession of a further twenty black specimens. Described as noiseless and resembling Old English Sheep dogs, only much larger with shaggy coats and big heads, the cyclist saw a profitable opportunity in grabbing one of the passing hounds to sell at Darlington Market, however after diving to capture one of the ethereal creatures he ended up in a bed of nettles...

An example of the Barghest breed of far more malevolent nature is the beast synonymous with Troller's Gill, the sinister limestone gorge near Appletreewick in Upper Wharfedale. Populated by trolls, sprites and flesh eating boggarts – for more detail of this glowing saucer eyed monster and the murderous miscreants who share his gorge see the entry under the letter 'T'.

Blue Stone, Holy Trinity Church, Wensley

There is a strange and old tradition observed in Holy Trinity Church, Wensley. Dating back at least a hundred years if not more, the custom concerns the 'Blue Stone', a large dark grave slab set into the floor of the nave. Actually the tomb stone commemorates two fifteenth century rectors of Wensley – brothers Richard and John Cledrow, yet a strange tradition is still observed in that both wedding and funeral parties must halt over the Blue Stone before proceeding to either get married or be buried. Nobody seems quite sure why or how such a ritual evolved, the only exception being the matrimony or burial of any of the Lords Bolton, whose family seat is at nearby Bolton Hall. In their case 'pass go' and proceed straight to the chancel!

The Blue Stone, Holy Trinity Church, Wensley

Burning Bartle, West Witton

To any casual visitor to Wensleydale or those merely passing through the National Park, the sturdy little settlement of West Witton with grey stone cottages strung along the northern facing lower slopes of Penhill seems no less distinctive than any other of the villages, hamlets or sprinkling of homesteads found on the road to Hawes, with the rolling scenery of Wensleydale unfolding on either side. There is however, concealed beneath the surface of everyday Witton life, the secret of a curious and some would say brutal ceremony which is annually re-enacted with a sacrificial parade culminating in a fiery crescendo – 'the Burning of Old Bartle'.

A true community occasion, the 'Witton Feast' is a weekend of village events beginning with the Cottage Show and the popular West Witton Fell

Race run over the upper crags of Penhill, however this is just the precursors to the real show stopper, a night time procession of some two hundred people following the progress of a gruesome Guy Fawkesesque effigy paraded down the main street before being consigned to a symbolic fiery death. The larger than life straw filled mannequin with a grisly masked face and light bulbs for eyes is, in accordance with long-standing tradition, constructed in secret by a local family some weeks prior to the parade which is always held on the Saturday nearest 24th August – St Bartholomew's Day. Carried by two bearers, and accompanied by a stick wielding 'caller' who repeatedly chants the 'Bartle Doggerel' on the progression through the village, around 9pm Bartle débuts near Kagram's Green Hill at the western end of the village where the initial merriment and drinking begins. The Doggerel, ritually recited at specific locations where the parade halts en route through the village is also the signal for the bearers to be rewarded with a drink or three!

> *On Penhill Crags he tore his rags*
> *Hunters Thorn he blew his horn*
> *Cappelbank Stee happened a misfortune and brak' his knee*
> *Grassgill Beck he brak' his neck*
> *Wadhams End he couldn't fend*
> *Grassgill End we'll mak' his end*
> *Shout, lads, shout!*

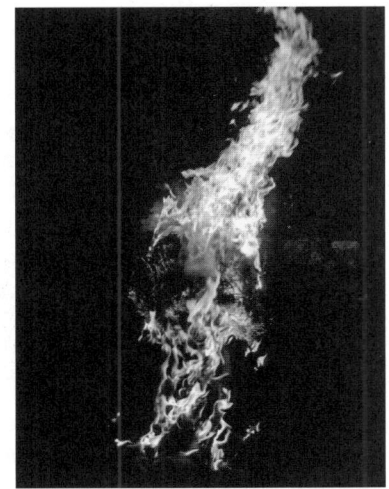

The blazing effigy of Bartle consumed by flames at Grassgill End

A definite high point of the Witton calendar, this remnant of ritualistic folklore has been re-enacted for hundreds of years, Bartle being variously identified as lynched sixteenth century livestock thief, a pre-Christian sun deity, even the bad old 'Giant of Penhill'. Whatever his ultimate origins are, Bartle in return brings prosperity wherever he goes, demonstrating a great generosity of spirit in view of the fiery fate repeatedly befalling him year after year in the flaming finale played out at Grassgill End where the Bartle effigy is anointed with a touch of accelerant and set ablaze to the general delight of the cheering crowd.

Busby Stoop Chair - Haunted Seat of Death, Thirsk Museum, Thirsk

The Busby Stoop Chair, or the 'Dead Man's Chair' as it is otherwise known is allegedly an old oak arm chair that was supposedly cursed by convicted murderer, Thomas Busby, prior to his execution opposite the pub that for so many years bore the name the Busby Stoop Inn.

Reputedly a drunkard, Thomas Busby was arrested, tried and condemned for the murder of his father-in-law Daniel Auty in 1702. Busby had snagged the hand of the village beauty Elizabeth Auty, though their marriage caused some considerable family frictions as Elizabeth's father was strongly opposed to the match. On returning home one evening Busby found Daniel Auty sitting in his favourite chair; Elizabeth's father declared he had come to take his daughter away, provoking Busby into a rage that later resulted in his strangling his father-in-law in bed that very night.

After his execution Busby's body was gibbeted at the Sand Hutton crossroads, and in a nod to the dead man's notoriety, the inn was renamed the Busby Stoop (the 'stoop' being the post from which he was hung).

The Busby Stoop Chair, mounted high up on the wall and safely out of bottom's reach!
Photographed with the kind permission of Thirsk Museum

However, before his execution Busby had cast a universal curse on all who deigned to sit in his favourite chair, and since Busby's initial curse was made a total of 63 people who had reportedly sat in the chair died shortly afterwards... Wartime bomber pilots from nearby RAF Skipton-on-Swale certainly thought the chair unlucky, and numbering amongst those unfortunates who supposedly succumbed to Busby's utterance were two airmen who died in car accident hours after taking a fateful seat, along with a furniture repairman called Carlo Pagnani.

After a number of fatal incidents in the 1970s linked to the chair, with a view to shaking off the sinister reputation gained by the inn, in 1978 the then landlord asked that the chair be removed once and for all. Ultimately hung from a high hook on the wall in Thirsk Museum preventing any further inadvertent or deliberate occupation, the Busby Stoop Chair remains an exhibit in the museum today.

For many years, as a reminder of Busby's murderous misdeed, a hangman's noose used to dangle from the exterior of the pub facing on to the Northallerton road. However, after a recent renovation (during which workmen experienced some inexplicable and presumably supernatural interference – it has long been held that Busby vociferously haunts the pub), the new owners, perhaps thinking that a noose displayed outside their establishment in poor taste, had the rope taken down along with the old pub sign depicting the fateful chair, and today the Busby Stoop gives no visible external clues as to sinister tradition once seated therein.

Buttertubs, near Hawes

The high, winding Buttertubs Pass connecting Wensleydale and Swaledale affords some of the grandest views of any high moorland route, and is a motoring enthusiasts dream. Rated by the redoubtable ex-presenter of one of television's most popular motoring shows as *'England's only truly spectacular road'*, the roadside crash barriers are reassuringly strengthened at the point where the dizzying drop into the valley below is separated by only yards of tarmac from the 65 foot deep group of fluted limestone potholes called the Buttertubs. The name is said to derive from the age old practice of farmers, resting after the steep climb on their way to market, who would lower the butter they had produced into the 'Buttertubs' to keep cool on a hot day. These once makeshift refrigerators are the dramatic result of thousands of years of erosion and certainly a very curious geological feature. An amusing anecdote attached to the Tubs runs along the lines that when asked how deep they were, one old farmer is said to have replied *'That one's bottomless... but over there is one that's even deeper!'*

The Buttertubs

21

C

Carperby's cross looking Cross, Carperby Village, Wensleydale

Harking back to the days when Carperby once held a market, in the centre of the village is a high stepped stone cross dated 1674. Carperby received its market charter in 1305, one of the earliest in the northern dales, permitting a weekly market and two annual fairs, one on St James Day in July and one on St Andrew's Day in November. There is some suggestion that this market may have fallen into disuse after 1587 when the neighbouring town of Askrigg was granted its own market charter, becoming the greater commercial focus in the upper dale. However Carperby's market was revived in the seventeenth century hence the carved date. The other more intriguing carvings on the cross are found on either end of each of the two horizontal cross arms – a pair of less than happy looking faces.

One of Carperby's pair of 'cross' faces

Castleshaw Tower, Sedbergh

Castlehaw Tower, or *Castlehaugh* as it is otherwise known, is a small well preserved motte and bailey castle on the north-eastern fringes of Sedbergh. Crowning an existing hill, the 30 foot high oval earth motte surrounded by a ditch still some 15 feet wide in places provided the perfect vantage point for surveillance of the entire valley and the opportunity of observing likely invaders approaching from any of those dales branching in along the valleys of the rivers Lune, Rawthey, Clough and Dee. In all probability the position was earlier utilised by the Romans as a look out post and signal station. Later the Normans topped and surrounded the modified mound with their distinctive brand of fortification – a typical castle of the period would have a wooden tower on the hill or motte, surrounded by a courtyard enclosed by a surrounding protective ditch and palisade – the bailey.

Castleshaw was possibly constructed at the behest of Alan de Mowbray, as Domesday Book tells us that Sedbergh was at that time held by the de Mowbray family. Centuries later, Castleshaw's marshal function was revived with the threat of attack from the skies; in World War II the mound was used as an as air raid look out manned by the Royal Observer Corps, though the original post had become operational in 1938, equipped with flares to warn friendly aircraft of nearby high ground. However in the face of the later Soviet nuclear threat precipitated by the advent of the Cold War many above ground posts were converted into underground bunkers, and Castleshaw was thus modified in 1965, though it only served as such for three years. It is haunting to think that Castleshaw was amongst one of several such Cold War observer posts built in the Yorkshire Dales National Park throughout this period of sustained political and military tension – terminated with the ultimate collapse of the USSR on 26th December 1991, when all Cold War defenses were finally stood down.

'Catch'em Corner', Darley, near Harrogate

In common with many other towns and villages around the UK, it is claimed that notorious highwayman Dick Turpin frequented Darley, the village some nine miles from Harrogate set between Birstwith and Dacre on the banks of the River Nidd. In fact a property on the Menwith Hill Road is still named 'Turpin's Lair', and the junction known as 'Catch'em Corner' supposedly refers to the times when Turpin held up and robbed many a stage coaches at this point, his activities curtailed by his flamboyant final performance on the gallows at York in 1739.

Cavendish Memorial, Bolton Abbey Estate, Wharfedale

Alongside the B6160 where the road passes through the Bolton Abbey Estate, part of the Duke of Devonshire's Yorkshire holdings, stands the Cavendish Memorial Fountain, built in honour of Lord Frederick Cavendish second son of the 7th Duke of Devonshire. Dated 1886 and bearing the inscription '*This fountain was erected by electors of the West Riding as a tribute to his memory, Frederick Charles Cavendish Born November XXX. MDCCCXXXVI. Died May VI. MDCCCLXXXII*' (that's born 30th November 1836 died 6th May 1882 for anyone needing to brush up on their Roman numerals!), this impressive hexagonal buttressed edifice commemorates the life of this English Liberal politician who was a protégé of Gladstone. Appointed Chief Secretary for Ireland in May 1882, Lord Frederick held the office for the briefest of times as he was murdered only hours after his arrival in Dublin.

Cheshire Cat, Croft-on-Tees

At Croft-on-Tees the lovely church of St Peter's is just a stone's throw from the river, and it is believed that a church has stood on the site since the ninth century. Apart from the charming setting, St Peter's main claim to fame is that Lewis Carroll's father came here as rector in 1843, Lewis eleven years old at the time. One of eleven brothers and sisters, Charles Lutwidge Dodgson (Lewis Carroll was his pen name) first started making up stories to entertain his family at Croft, and it is said that much of *Alice in Wonderland* was inspired by settings in and around the rectory and church.

Carroll's inspiration for the 'Cheshire Cat'?

The well known character of the 'Cheshire Cat' may well have been drawn from the carved stone face of a cat or lion adorning the sedilla – a seat for clergy built into the wall – as when viewed from a forward pew the broad smile is clear, however on standing the cheesy grin seems to disappear, much as the vanishing Cheshire Cat's did. (More of Carroll's ecclesiastic inspirations can be found under the letter 'Q'.)

Carroll also wrote the first verse of his famous nonsense poem "Jabberwocky" at Croft, attributed by some to tales of the Sockburn Worm, a ferocious dragon like creature said in days of yore to have laid waste to the nearby village of Sockburn, where according to legend around the time of the Norman Conquest a huge man-eating dragon with poisonous breath, sometimes described as a wyrm, wyvern or flying serpent, was terrorising the village. Now comprising of a ruined church, a farmhouse and a mansion called Sockburn Hall (built in 1834) all positioned within a loop in the River Tees known locally as the Sockburn Peninsula, the then lord of the manor Sir John Conyers took up the challenge to slay the beast. Successful in his quest, the Grey Stone standing in a field near the ruined church still marks the place of battle and burial spot of the Sockburn Worm.

Even though it is said that Carroll wrote the poem as a parody designed to show how *not* to write a poem, it is considered by many to be one of the greatest nonsense poems written in the English language.

Christian Crustaceans, Masham

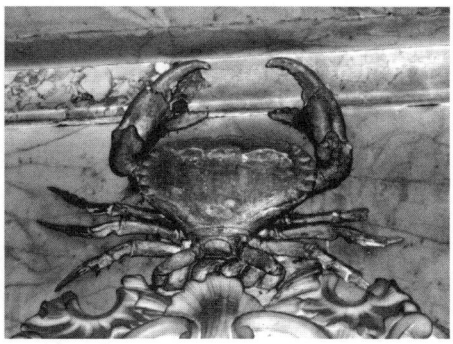

One of the 'Christian Crustaceans' in St Mary's Church, Masham

In the beautiful St Mary's Church in Masham various tombs and memorials mark the resting places of members of the Scrope family who established themselves in lower Wensleydale in the twelfth century. The heraldic golden crabs seen emerging from the ducal coronets adorning the family's monuments around the church are part of the crest of the Lords Scrope of Masham. Derived in part from their family motto *'Devant si je puis'* – 'Forward if I am able', a nod to the crab's habitual sideways scuttle, this heraldic emblem may also be a sardonic allusion to the family name, Scrope translating to 'crab' in the Norman French, or the crab being called a 'scrap' in northern dialect, to date I have found four of these delightful creatures in St Mary's Church – there may be more...

Churn Stand, Butterset, near Hawes

Up until the first half of the twentieth century churn stands would have been a familiar sight all around the country, especially in areas where dairying was commonplace, and in some parts of the Yorkshire Dales National Park there may literally have been a churn stand for every farm.

Not such a frequent site these days, tanker collections directly from milking parlour storage tanks as opposed to loading the churns off of a stone stand into the back of a horse-drawn cart, along with new regulations governing milk transportation made the churn stand an obsolete feature.

Back in the day, the milk that was collected from the Dales would often be taken to one of the larger dairies, in Hawes, Skipton or even as far afield as Leeds. The milk collected from the Burtersett stand may have been destined for one of the cheese factories in Hawes, or onto the 'milk train' which ran from Hawes Station to York up until the 1950s.

Some of those stone stands not dismantled for reuse in other building projects have found a second lease of life in a variety of different purposes however, from handy platforms on which to sell roadside produce to podiums for proud gardeners to exhibit flourishing displays.

Coffin Stone, Corpse Way, Ivelet Bridge near Gunnerside, Swaledale

Closely associated with the legendary canine harbinger of death the 'Headless Hound of Ivelet Bridge' mentioned under the letter 'B' for 'Barguests', the Coffin Stone is a flat horizontal slab set into the verge on the north side of the hump-backed Ivelet Bridge. Just wide enough to accommodate one car crossing the River Swale, over this single arched bridge the 'Corpse Way' passes, a 16-mile path travelled until the late sixteenth century by the villagers of Keld forced to carry the bodies of the deceased all the way to Grinton as here was the only consecrated ground for burial in the upper dale. A very necessary journey bearing in mind that in medieval times if you weren't buried in hallowed soil then your soul would be damned for all eternity, along the route are a number of long flat flagstones where the wicker coffin would have been set down while the funeral party rested, and the 'Coffin Stone' at Ivelet Bridge is one such place where weary pall bearers could rest their 'dead weight'. This potentially hazardous two day journey, especially in winter (there are records of pall bearers being swept away while trying to ford the flooded river at other points), incorporated an overnight stop at the Punchbowl Inn at Low Row where the corpse would be stored in the imaginatively named 'Dead House'. However, after the consecration of a chapel of ease and graveyard at Muker in 1580 the dead from the top of the dale no longer had to make their final journey down the Corpse Way, which today is a popular route for walkers enjoying some spectacular scenery.

Ivelet Bridge – The Coffin Stone, now somewhat obscured by overgrowth is set into the verge on the far side of the gate

Conjuring Stone, Aldwark

If approaching the village of Aldwark from the south, the expense of the 40 pence toll to cross the bridge reputed to have been damaged by an iceberg in the 19th century is well worth the outlay as this will save a 25 mile detour. With regard to the Curiosity, in the village of Aldwark is a satanic legacy, the 'Conjuring Stone', beneath which the imprisoned spirit known as the Witch of Hollows Hole is '*doomed for a certain time to walk the night, and for the day confined to fast in fires, till the foul crimes done in his days of nature be burned and purged away*'. Exorcised by a priest long ago, this troublesome spirit was pinioned under the Conjuring Stone to prevent his wandering and haunting the neighbourhood – the Stone today lies within the private grounds of the Aldwark Manor Hotel, presumably with expunged wizard still in situ.

Cow & Calf Rocks, Ilkley Moor

The well known bovine boulders of the Cow and Calf Rocks are a millstone grit outcrop formation high on Ilkley Moor. Also known as Hangingstone Rocks, the Cow and Calf are so named as the larger stone with the smaller sat next to it are said to be reminiscent of a mother cow and her young. Legend has it that at one time there was also a 'bull' rock in existence, but that it was quarried away for building material as Ilkley grew into a fashionable Victorian spa town. There is however another legend accounting for the Cow and Calf that tells of the giant Rombald (giants seem to make a frequent appearance in the folklore of the Yorkshire Dales), who on fleeing from his angry wife stamped on the rocks as he leapt across the valley and split the Calf from Cow. In pursuit, the incensed Mrs Rombald dropped all the stones she had been carrying in her skirts creating yet another rock formation aptly known as 'The Skirtful of Stones'.

The Cow and Calf Rocks, Ilkley Moor courtesy of Snapshots Of The Past

An abundance of other curious stones litter the vicinity, Rombald's Moor boasting the second highest concentration of ancient carved stones in Europe, including the 'Badger Stone' and 'Panorama Rocks' dating from the late Neolithic and Bronze Ages as well as the 'Swastika Stone' on Woodhouse Crag, the design, possibly of Roman origin, unique to the British Isles.

Craven Heifer

The Craven Heifer is a pub name that appears throughout the Dales, and the inn so named in Addingham particularly apt as the village is just three miles south of Bolton Abbey, birthplace of the original bounteous bovine.

Bred by the Reverend W Carr in 1807 on the Duke of Devonshire's Bolton Abbey estate, the Craven Heifer was fed relentlessly until reaching her peak and weighing an immense 312 Stone 8 lbs and measuring 11 feet and 4 inches from nose to rump. This massive short-horn cow became something of a celebrity in her own right and was understandably the wonder of farmers from all over England, famous enough not only to be featured on inn signs, her image also appeared on some of the notes issued by the Craven Bank.

Purchased by a Mr John Watkinson of Halton East in 1811 for the sum of £200, being such a fine animal she was taken down to Smithfield to exhibit, the journey from Wakefield to London taking 73 days from 19th November to 30th January. Shown off at numerous towns and cities en route, presumably her propensity toward plumpness kept out the winter chill...

Sadly, the magnificent Craven Heifer met an ignoble end when she was put up and won as a prize in a cockfight, sold off at a few pence a pound..

Culloden Tower, Richmond

Standing in a splendid position with views over the treetops to the town of Richmond and surrounding countryside this octagonal folly was built in 1746 to celebrate the defeat of Bonnie Prince Charlie, Scottish pretender to the English throne. Aptly named for the decisive battle in which George II's son Prince William Augustus had earnt the brutal sobriquet of 'Butcher Cumberland', the Battle of Culloden saw the decimation of the Scottish army in the final and decisive confrontation of the 1745 Jacobite uprising.

The octagonal gothic folly Culloden Tower, Richmond

Following the fashion for Gothic follies, the Tower was built by Whig politician John Yorke on the ruins of Hudswell Tower, a former Pele tower (one of many small fortified keeps built along the English and Scottish borders) which had stood on the spot from the fourteenth century until it was demolished in the 1730s. The purpose of the 'new' tower was however a decorative one, set in the landscaped parkland of Yorke House. Now in the possession of the Landmark Trust, the splendid Culloden Tower is available as an usual holiday retreat.

D

Dead Man's Hill, Arkleside, near Horsehouse, Coverdale

Travelling the old packhorse road running from Middlesmoor in Nidderdale, before part of the route was submerged beneath the waters of Scar House Reservoir, the way passed over the summit of the aptly named Dead Man's Hill. It is said hereabouts that the headless, vengeful wraiths of three murdered Scottish peddlers restlessly patrol the high ground separating Coverdale from Nidderdale, their decapitated bodies having been discovered here in 1728. Presumed murdered at a wayside inn in the now ruined hamlet of Lodge overlooking the reservoir, the finger of suspicion was firmly pointed in the direction of the landlady and her daughter. Further embroidering of the tale lending additional weight to the culpability of the murderous innkeeping pair alludes to their apparent inexplicable increase in wealth, with rumours abounding that they ensnared their victims with sexual favours, enticing their return only to murder the peddlers for their full purses.

Legend still links the wicked mother and daughter with the pair of stone outcrops on the moor above Ramsgill, some 5 miles to the northeast of Dead Man's Hill and know as Jenny Twigg and her daughter Tib – for more of these malevolent rock representations said to have been turned to stone as punishment for their misdoings see their entry under the letter 'J'.

Dead Man's Hill, seen from the Nidderdale approach across Scar House Reservoir

Death's Scythe, St Mary's churchyard, Barnard Castle

Adjoining the now ruined castle that gave rise to the town's name, in the graveyard of the twelfth century St Mary's church rests George Hopper of Black Hedley who died aged 23 in 1725. Formerly buried inside the church near the west end of the south aisle, since the tomb was removed outside, the carvings on two sides of the table style monument are now somewhat weathered but still apparent. On the north facing (church facing side) is the depiction of a young man in early eighteenth century garb; once vividly painted, clearly the pigments intended to better weather the test of time had the monument not been exposed to the elements. The inscription on this side runs '*Here stands my statue carved in Stone To mind ye living I am gone*'. However on the southern side of Hopper's monument, facing on to the churchyard, the wording '*He cometh forth like a flower and is cut down*' accompanies the somewhat more grisly carved representation of Death, a skeleton holding a scythe. Have a care not to gaze too long however, as it is this carving of a somewhat knock-kneed cadaver that holds the sinister portent of doom, as in accordance with locally held belief, to see Death's scythe *move* foretells of foreboding and ill fortune soon to befall anyone foolhardy enough to sustain their stare.

Devilish diversification in the Dales!
No entry under the letter 'D' would be complete without mention of the Devil. Prolific in his creation of ditches, dykes, punch bowls, quoits and cheesewrings, Old Nick must have been continually busy leaving his mark on the landscape of our British Isles, however where the Yorkshire Dales are concerned there's no indication of his putting his satanic hooves up as evidence of his devilish antics are evident throughout the landscape and folklore of the Dales…

Devil's Arrows, Boroughbridge
We begin the litany of Beelzebub's bequests to the Dales with the Devil's Arrows, three huge standing stones, or menhir, on the western outskirts of Boroughbridge. Thought to originally have numbered five, the fourth stone was reputedly broken up in 1582 by treasure hunters, and according to tradition the top of this stone was to be found in the grounds of Aldborough Hall while the rest of it ended up in the fabric of Peg Bridge which crosses the River Tutt as it enters the town. As for the fifth stone – who knows? Some suggestion has been made that the stones were erected by the Romans to commemorate a great victory (there is a strong consensus that the northern province known as Britannia Inferior was centered on neighbouring village of Aldborough, or Isurium Brigantum to give the village its Roman name). However, the Arrows are known to date from the late Neolithic or Early Bronze Age period, and it is believed that the stones were once the site of a solstice fair with several astronomical alignments postulated, the southernmost summer moonrise being one, as well as a connection with a Ley Line alignment.

The stones have been known by other names through the ages, variously

Two of the Devil's Arrows - the third remaining Arrow stands on the other side of Roecliffe Lane in a fenced enclosure

the Devil's Bolts, the Three Greyhounds and the Three Sisters, but the story giving rise to the Arrows epithet seems to date back to an account first recorded in 1721 where Satan, annoyed by some bad word of mouth on the part of the inhabitants of Aldborough threw the stones at the village from his vantage point on How Hill (south of Fountains Abbey). Clearly his accuracy failing, the 'arrows' fell short by something of a mile and planted in the earth where they stand today. In a superstitious hark back to the Arrow's satanic origin, it was also claimed that to walk round the stones twelve times withershins, that's anti-clockwise, will raise the Devil!

Devil's Mustard Mill, Stenkrith Bridge, Kirkby Stephen
At the furthermost reaches of the Dales where the fells of the Lake District are met, formerly in the old county of Westmorland and surrounded by sparsely populated hill country is the ancient market town of Kirkby Stephen. Here one of the local myths handed down from generation to generation for hundreds of years pertains to the Devil's taste for hot mustard! While one would assume that Hell would be warm enough already, it is said that at

Stenkrith Bridge the sound of the labouring damned crushing mustard seeds for Mephistopheles can be heard if one places an ear to the rocks hereabouts. While there is a geological explanation - the waters of the River Eden flowing over the strange circular holes hollowed out by pebbles that have been swirled around by the river for millennia accounting for the low rumbling noise, still the centuries old tradition persists...

Devil's Bridges

Renowned for his prolific bridge building, there are a number of 'Devil's Bridges' in the Dales, probably the most notable to be found at Kirkby Lonsdale. This beautiful triple arched twelfth century bridge spans the River Lune, and is now a regular Sunday morning meeting place for motorbike enthusiasts (Hell's Angels I hear you ask?) The demonic legend associated with the bridge involves a woman who had been separated from her cow by the rising River Lune in flood – she supposedly made a pact with the Devil that if he would build her a bridge, in return she would surrender up the soul of the first living thing to cross over. The Devil obliged, but the woman out-witted Satan by inducing her dog to run across the bridge first, consequently the disgruntled Prince of Darkness was cheated of a human soul. Still to this day, if one peers over the edge of the bridge, beneath the arches you can see a large rock with a hole in it – the 'Devil's Neck Collar' – lost from Satan's neck when he plunged from the bridge after being tricked out of his prize.

The Devil's Bridge at Kirkby Lonsdale

In Dibbledale the River Dibb, one of England's shortest rivers, flows out from Grimwith Reservoir and down under Dibble's Bridge, supposedly built by the Devil in a moment of rare generosity toward a

Kilgram Bridge minus the cursed missing stone

local shoemaker who shared a drink with him. Nearby at Howgill we also find 'The Devil's Apronful', a cairn supposedly the result of a satanic trip-up when, determined to fill up the Dibble ravine (or perhaps carrying the foundations for the shoemaker's bridge) the Devil caught his foot on the top of Nursa Knott and stumbling, dropping his load of rock on the ground where they still lay today. Incidentally Dibble is not a corruption of the Devil at all but comes from the old English 'dybbel' meaning 'bridge over the pool'; perhaps then the satanic story arose to account for the curious name, the true meaning of which had long since been forgotten.

Yet another of the Devil's bridges can be found between Middleham and Masham where Kilgram Lane crosses over the River Ure. Traditionally marking the lower end of Wensleydale, beneath this ancient span is the much older and still visible paved Roman ford, one of the best preserved in Britain. While the medieval ribbed arches are believed to be the have been built by in the early twelfth century by Cistercian monks who founded nearby Jervaulx Abbey, legend attributes the construction of Kilgram Bridge to the Devil after a pact was made with the local populace. To this day superstition holds that a satanic curse will fall on anyone attempting to replace the missing stone from the upstream facing side of the bridge... Those in the mood for casual bridge repair – you have been warned!

At our final Satanic span, Lucifer certainly left his cloven stamp with the apt naming of Hell Gill Bridge in the lovely Mallerstang. Crossing over Hell Gill Beck, on the old Wensleydale to Eden Valley fell tops highway, antiquarian John Leland's allusion to the 'hellish' associations of this bridge date back to the sixteenth century when he wrote of *'a Bek called Hell Gill because it runnithe in such a deadley place'*. Before reaching Hell Gill Bridge, the Beck plunges into a narrow, deep gorge where legend maintains that Dick Turpin, on one of his many reputed escapades, leapt across the chasm and in so doing crossed the county border and escaped his pursuers. A small stone incorporated into one of the parapets of the 'new' Hell Gill Bridge built in 1825 is thought to be the old boundary stone that marked the borders of Yorkshire and the historic county of Westmorland.

Dickens real life Dotheboys Hall, Bowes

Bowes, a quiet village some four miles from Barnard Castle lays claim to having inspired Charles Dickens, generally regarded as the greatest novelist of the Victorian period, in his creation of Dotheboys Hall, the brutish establishment in his novel Nicholas Nickleby where *'boys were taken in and done for by a Mr. Squeers, a puffing, ignorant, over-bearing brute, who starved them and taught them nothing'*. Today a wooden plaque identifies the former academy where the one time master William Shaw, supposedly the real life model for the sadistic schoolmaster Wackford Squeers, held sway over his wretched charges. Shaw died in 1850, and is buried in St Giles churchyard, along with George Ashton Taylor, whose grave provided Dickens with the further inspiration for the character of Smike, the schoolboy who was so badly treated by the wicked one-eyed Squeers.

Drummer Boy's Stone, footpath to Easby Abbey, Richmond

A well-famed and noisy child ghost is incorporated into the many legends associated with Richmond Castle, the impressive ruin of one of the Conqueror's defenses perched in a commanding position above the River Swale. The famous and widely known story of the 'Drummer Boy' tells of an unfortunate lad lowered into the mouth of a newly discovered passageway that the soldiers garrisoned at Richmond believed linked the castle to nearby Easby Abbey. He was told to beat his drum in order that the subterranean route could be marked out by the listening soldiers following his progress above ground, but midway the sound of drumming ceased... and the little drummer boy never emerged. Even after several centuries it is said that his drum beats can still be heard as he makes his way along the mysterious lost tunnel, and on the footpath between castle and abbey is the 'Drummer Boy's Stone', a monument with a plaque reading:

> 'According to legend, this stone marks the spot where the Richmond drummer boy reached in the tunnel supposed to lead from Richmond Market Place to Easby Abbey. Here the sound of his drumming ceased and he was never seen again.'

E

Earthquakes

Though the UK is not particularly prone to earthquakes, our island does experience between 20-30 seismic events every year that are of sufficient magnitude to cause notice. In the Yorkshire Dales, *Pennine shudders* arise from the fault in the Askrigg Block, an underlying granite mass butting up against the Craven and Dent Faults, and it was one such tremor at 9pm on the evening of Wednesday 5th January 2011 that propelled the village of Kirkby Malzeard into the national spotlight as the epicentre of an earthquake measuring 3.6 on the Richter Scale.

Felt in homes across the North-East and North Yorkshire, though thankfully only minor damage resulted, the Kirkby Malzeard tremor was the most powerful in the area since the quake reverberating through Wensleydale on 9th December 1780, this one measuring 4.8 on the Richter Scale. The upper end of Wensleydale is clearly a prominent centre of repeated seismic activity as other significant earthquakes were experience in 1768, 1871, 1933 and 1970. By global standards, the Kirkby Malzeard event was not exactly earth shattering, but likely to leave a lasting impression upon those who saw their flagstone floors 'dance'!

Easby Cross, St Agatha's Church, Easby Abbey, near Richmond

The abbey church of St Agatha at Easby is famed for its thirteenth century wall paintings, and rightly so as they are probably the finest collection in North Yorkshire. These breathtaking depictions on the north wall of the chancel draw on subjects from the Old Testament, while those on the south wall are taken from the New Testament, the paintings laid on the walls over 600 years ago while the plaster was still wet.

St Agatha's also boast a plaster replica of the Easby Cross, the carved stone original now in the the Victoria and Albert Museum. Though the Easby Cross is an example of early Christiananity pushing out Celtic heathen monuments, the Celtic carved designs were however carried over and applied to many Christian crosses, and inspite of the intricate intertwining knotwork decorating the Easby Cross, it is ironic that the indirect survival of the Cross was a consequence of its perceived crude appearance; broken up and used as convenient building material in the new church, by inadvertently incorporating the Cross fragments into the fabric of the church walls, the Easby Cross was protected over the centuries until more appreciative antiquarians pieced it back together again in 1930.

Ebbing and Flowing Well, Giggleswick

Situated at the foot of Giggleswick Scar beside the road running from Settle to Clapham is the ancient and magical 'Ebbing and Flowing Well'. A place used for prophecy and divination in times past, the waters of the well do in fact periodically ebb and flow, sometimes brimming over on to the road and at other times being at least 8 feet below the edge of the stone trough into which the well waters run. Though no conclusive cause for the water's rise and fall can be established, there is a legend of a water nymph, pursued by a lusty satyr, whose imploring prayers were answered when the gods transformed her into the fabric of the well, thus evading the

Vestige of early Christianity, the Easby Cross

satyr's saucy clutches, the tidal ebbs and flows of the water said to be caused by her eternal breath. A charming story, unfortunately the Ebbing and Flowing Well no longer sinks and rises with breathy regularity since the rhythm of this phenomenon was interrupted by the misguided excavation of the well many years ago. In an attempt to ascertain the reason for this curious characteristic, sadly in spite of replacing all of the stones exactly as they had been found, the investigative work destroyed the very essence of what it had been undertaken to discover... Today the well has been reduced to a rather more erratic performance, but is still a marvel nonetheless, and perhaps an endorsement to the old adage 'if it ain't broke, don't fix it'...

Edwin and Emma, Ballad of the Bowes Tragedy

The Ancient Unicorn in Bowes is a former coaching inn able to trace it's history back to the sixteenth century when the Stainmore Pass (now the A66) was an important trade route. The inn is also renowned as the haunt (literally) of 'Edwin and Emma', the doomed lovers whose story was poetically immortalised in the ballad 'The Bowes Tragedy'.

Edwin and Emma (or Roger Wrightson and Martha Ritson to give them their real names) were both from local inn keeping families – Roger's kept the Kings' Head, now the Bowes Working Men's Club and Martha's family the Unicorn. The couple fell in love in 1713, but the match faced some stiff parental objection on the part of the Wrightsons; feeling they were socially a cut above the Ritsons, the young lovers were forced to meet in secret. Their year long hidden romance was cut short however when Roger fell seriously ill with fever on Shrove Tuesday 1714. As he neared death, his parents relented

The Ancient Unicorn, Bowes, haunt of Edwin and Emma

and allowed Martha to see her love one last time, Roger dying three days later. Martha in her turn died shortly afterwards it is said from a broken heart, but the two were ultimately united as they were buried together at the west end of St Giles churchyard, though clearly not ultimately at rest, as rising from this shared grave the ghosts of 'Edwin and Emma' have regularly been seen haunting the Ancient Unicorn.

Capitalising on the story of the star-crossed spooks, by 1717 the master of Bowes Grammar School had penned the 23 verse ballad variously entitled 'The Pattern of True Love' or 'The Bowes' Tragedy', and it is said that Martha's younger sister, Tamar, made a reasonable living well into her old age singing the verses to travellers passing through Bowes.

St Giles churchyard also boast two other noteworthy burials – see the letter 'D' for 'Dickens Real Life Dotheboys Hall'.

Elgar Connection, Giggleswick, Settle

The English composer Edward Elgar (1857-1934), whose many works have entered the British and international classical concert repertoire, was a regular visitor to the Yorkshire Dales. Elgar loved the informality of Dales life, enjoying walks in the area where the limestone scars, becks and waterfalls so differed from his beloved Malvern Hills, drawing inspiration from the

Plaque commemorating Elgar's stays in Settle, affixed to Dr Buck's former surgery on the Market Place, now the NatWest Bank

countryside to compose his most famous works – the *Enigma Variations* and *Pomp and Circumstance*. On many occasions he stayed in Settle with his good friend Dr Charles William Buck and there is a blue plaque commemorating Elgar's visits to what was once Buck's surgery, now on the façade of the branch of National Westminster Bank in Settle Market Place. Though Buck's surgery was in Settle, his home was in the neighbouring village of Giggleswick and it was in the back room of the house here, dedicated as a music room, that Elgar found time to compose while sojourning in the Yorkshire Dales. Invariably signing his locally-composed scores with the annotation '*Giggleswyke*', some forgotten Elgarian compositions written at Dr Buck's house in 1882 were discovered in a farm house in the Lake District stored in the case of a grandfather clock! Though so different from his native Worcestershire, Elgar must have held many fond associations with Giggleswick as in 1888 on one of his visits he composed the short violin and piano piece entitled *Salut d'Amour* which he presented as an engagement present to his fiance and future wife Alice.

Eloy – a unique saintly dedication, Great Smeaton, near Northallerton

Standing on the site of Great Smeaton's earlier eleventh century Saxon church, St Eloy's is unique in it's dedication as it is the only church in England dedicated to the 'Blacksmith's Saint'. Though a common dedication in France, this patron saint of goldsmiths, blacksmiths and all workers in metal was perhaps appropriated for Great Smeaton as the village name is thought to derive from the Anglo-Saxon word *Smideton* meaning the 'smith's farm'.

Also known as the Patron Saint of horses, there is a legend attached to St Eloy concerning his shoeing of a horse possessed by the Devil. Though the creature was quite uncontrollable, Eloy simply cut off one of the horse's forelegs and re-shod the hoof on the amputated leg before miraculously re-attaching it to the horse. It is thought that the fragmentary remnant of a medieval wall painting in another Dales church, Wensley's Holy Trinity, depicts this incredible act of farriering where on the north wall of the nave a suitably devilish-looking horse grins malevolently above a figure wearing what seem to be clerical vestments, wielding a hammer ready to shoe the demonic horse.

Eroded Exhibitionist, Copgrove's Saucy Sheel-na-gig

Located in the unlikely environs of the church of St Michael and All Angels in Copgrove some six mile south of Ripon, incorporated into the interior fabric of the nave wall close to the pulpit is the eroded yet explicit Copgrove Sheel-na-gig. Typically such architectural grotesques featuring figurative carvings of a naked women were said to ward off evil spirits, a function this lady may well have performed in her original alfresco position when she was built into the exterior fabric of the north chancel wall. Thought to be of Romano-British origin, the now badly worn stone was moved inside the church to prevent further erosion by the Yorkshire elements, though her weathered state now obscures what could be politely described as a gynecologically exaggerated motif! As mentioned in the Easby Cross entry, the introduction of Christianity to many places of former pagan worship was often smoothed by the incorporation of primitive pre-christian symbolism into the fabric of the new church, therefore the Copgrove carving could have been representative of a Celtic fertility or mother goddess, later co-opted as a cautionary depiction of corrupting female lust, the sin of Eve omnipresent since the beginnings of Christianity. Whatever her origins, one can say with certainty that the Copgrove Sheel-na-gig is definitely an exhibitionist!

St Eloy – half saint/half farrier – about to shoe a demonic grinning horse in one of the medieval wall paintings preserved in Wensley Church

The Copgrove Sheel-na-gig carving

F

Fairy Well, Harmby

The Fairy Well, located in open pasture just to the west of Harmby village, has the distinction of being marked on the first edition Ordnance Survey map for the area dating to around 1850, yet the well's connection with the 'Wee Folk' goes back far beyond this date...

While the water from the nearby spring has since been piped away, the Fairy Well continues to flow and livestock still drink from the cast iron trough that replaced the much older stone one now hidden beneath a collapsed dry-stone wall. Yet amongst this jumble of stones the spring supply can still be seen flowing from beneath a flat stone set into the side of the bank.

Growing alongside the Fairy Well are two old Hawthorn trees and an Elder tree, both types of tree having a place in folklore, the Elder especially linked with the faeries. Ancient fables also suggest that faerie folk don't much care for iron, and that any iron object could be employed to break a fairy spell. In the past, livestock that became sick for no obvious reason were often thought to have been 'elf shot', so perhaps the iron trough replacing the stone original was a protective measure to safeguard the herd from any enchantment...

The Fairy Well also overlooks the floodplain of the River Ure as it wends it's way past Middleham toward Jervaulx Abbey, and in the past such low lying land was thought to be the haunt of 'Will-o-Wisps' or 'fairy lights', seen floating slowly across the ground on damp, misty nights and possibly lending more credence to the presence of Fairies in the vicinity of the well.

False February Tombstone, Fewston Churchyard

Fewston's church, with its dual dedication to St Michael and St Lawrence, is one of the very few seventeenth century churches in Yorkshire, the old medieval church having been rebuilt in 1696 after a devastating fire. Amongst the weather worn monuments in the sloping churchyard which in springtime is a riot of vibrant bluebells, is the curious grave of one Joseph Ridsdale and his son William. Though on first inspection the stone seems unremarkable, on closer scrutiny the curiosity is revealed; according to the carved inscription Joseph Ridsdale died on the 29th of February 1823, however this was not a leap year. But even more curious is the inscription for his son William, who apparently predeceased his father on the *30th* of February 1802. To this day

The tombstone in Fewston churchyard inscribed with not one but two curious February dating discrepancies

no-one knows the reason for the dating discrepancies; the only instance of a 30th February was that recorded in Sweden in 1712 due to a Gregorian calendar malfunction, and certainly not applicable to a village on the fringe of the Dales.

Fearby's Lost Stone Circle

Since Feraby's first mention as *Federbi* in the Domesday Book, the population has swelled somewhat from the eight villagers and one smallholder recorded in 1086 – but not much!

Looking further back at the history of this lovely little village, set either side of the road running through an expansive green, long before Domesday there are clues harking back to Neolithic Fearby reflected in the telling name of three adjoining fields known as 'Standing Stones'. Though nothing visibly remains today, Edmund Boggs who was a prolific writer of north-country guidebooks in the early 1900s mentions that between Fearby and the neighbouring hamlet of Healey "*there were formerly circles of upright stones and other relics suggestive of druidical origin*". In the earlier *History of Mashamshire* local author John Fisher alluded to circles of upright stones having '*recently existed*' near Healey, and he was writing in 1865. Fisher also referenced neighbouring Healey's associations with the ancient sun god Baal, and though the conclusions he drew based on interpretations of local place names – particularly *Healey-Baals* and *Baal Hill* – may have been convenient to his sun god suppositions, nevertheless Fisher also included some pertinent folklore relating to the local tradition of quarterly fire ceremonies celebrated hereabouts that he naturally linked to the now vanished Fearby Stone Circle:

"There are traditions, too, which have been handed down to us, to the effect that the heathen custom of making feasts and Baal-fires (which although unknown to the persons making them, were in truth so made in honour of Baal)

have been continued until very recent times in this district — and especially in Nidderdale — the remembrance of which is transmitted to us in the annual feast which is still held at Healey... This supposition is strengthened by the circumstance of circles of upright stones having recently existed near to the place, and from ancient relics which have been found within the parish, and at but a short distance from Healey and Healey-Baals, which are supposed to have been used in the mystical rites of the Druids or priests of Britain, for at least antiquaries can assign no other use to them..."

However, the only vestige of any fire festivals surviving today are perhaps to be found in the odd back garden bonfire or out of control BBQ!

Fertility Stone, near Pateley Bridge

This intriguingly named stone shares a common characteristic with many other 'cup and ring' carved rocks in the region (a form of prehistoric art found mainly in Atlantic Europe), invariably placed in positions affording extensive views out across the surrounding country, as the Fertility Stone is found on the higher ground overlooking the valley of the River Nidd,

While the specific naming of this stone is probably associated with local folklore indicating the magical properties the rock was mythically imbued with, even echoing a prehistoric use, some have speculated that the name of the Fertility Stone perhaps harks back to the beliefs of superstitious cattle owners, encouraging their stock to walk over the stone in the belief that it would increase the fertility of the herd. Built into the base of a tumbled down drystone wall, the carvings are now somewhat eroded, repeatedly trampled by the hooves of passing cattle who use the gap in the wall as a gateway. However, in spite of its worn state there is reason to believe that the Fertility Stone is still being exploited for it's supposed magical qualities today... and not just for bovine breeding purposes!

Fewston's Real Life Amos Barton

After the publication of *The Sad Fortunes of the Reverend Amos Barton* in 1857, author George Eliot (the masculine pen name adopted by Mary Ann Evans to ensure her works would be taken seriously) was forced to make an apology to the Reverend John Gwyther whose personal traits she had woven into her literary creation of Barton in a less than complimentary way.

Gwyther had been the local curate in Chilvers Coton, Eliot's childhood home, and had memorably officiated at the wedding of Eliot's sister in 1832, and the episode in Chapter one where Amos Barton rudely interrupts the wedding psalm was an incident drawn from life.

The tomb of John Gwyther, Vicar of Fewston and George Eliot's real life 'Amos Barton'

An advocate of Evangelical reform, after spells of incumbancy in Birmingham, Warwickshire and Sheffield, Gwyther became Vicar of St Michael and St Lawrence in Fewston, incumbent until his death in 1873. What Fewston's parishioners thought of the 'real life' Amos Barton is not on record, although the congregation showed no reserve in their opinion of Gwyther's successor, the Reverend John Marks Ashley. A classical scholar, he was said to be able '*to talk well but that is not what is wanted here*'.

The Reverend Gwyther's tomb stands beside the church porch, and shares the lofty graveyard overlooking Swinsty Reservoir with the 'False February Tombstone' mentioned above.

First Post – Frenchgate's Victorian Pillar Box, Richmond

This lovely hexagonal Victorian pillar box is sited at the southern end of Frenchgate in the centre of the dales town of Richmond, and a rarity as only 150 of the original Penfold designed boxes still remain in the UK. Distinguished by their hexagonal construction and Acanthus bud surmounting the cap, between 1866 and 1879 the hexagonal Penfold became the standard design for pillar boxes and it was during this period that red was first adopted as the standard colour, earlier Victorian boxes painted green so as not to appear too obtrusive in the landscape.

So effective was this camouflage however that complaints were received by people having difficulty finding them; the Post Office investigated alternative colours and

Frenchgate's Penfold design Victorian Pillar Box

initially settled on chocolate brown, however as this colour choice required an extra coat of varnish it proved more expensive and the alternative suggestion of bright red was adopted. Consequently the new colour was introduced in 1874, and it took 10 years to complete the programme of re-painting; ever since red has remained the standard colour for pillar boxes with few exceptions.

The Frenchgate pillar box and others of its ilk must have been welcome additions as prior to the introduction of letter boxes there were two principal ways of posting a letter – senders would either have to take the letter in person to a Receiving House (effectively an early Post Office) or would have to wait for the Bellman, a uniformed official who walked the streets collecting letters from the public, ringing a bell to attract attention. Think on this next time you grumble to yourself about having to go and post a letter!

Fox's Pulpit, Firbank, near Sedbergh

It was on the undulating ridges of Firbank Fellside a few miles from Sedbergh that George Fox, the founder of the Religious Society of Friends or Quakers, was encouraged to preach to a large gathering of 'Seekers', coming fresh from his revelatory vision on Pendle Hill. As Fox refused to go into the chapel to preach (as a 'non-conformists' Fox had separated himself from the mainstream forms of Christanity, and refrained from entering orthodox places of worship) he spoke instead for three hours to the gathered crowd from the top of a near by crag, the spot now immortalised as Fox's Pulpit, and considered by some as marking the beginning of the Friends Movement.

In Fox's words, at the end of Whitsun week, 1652 *'While others were gone to dinner, I went to a brook, got a little water, and then came and sat down on the top of a rock hard by the chapel. In the afternoon the people gathered about me, with several of their preachers. It was judged there were above a thousand people; to whom I declared God's everlasting truth and Word of life freely and largely for about the space of three hours.'*

A plaque on the rock there commemorates the event with the inscription:

> LET YOUR LIVES SPEAK
> HERE OR NEAR THIS ROCK GEORGE FOX PREACHED
> TO ABOUT ONE THOUSAND SEEKERS FOR THREE
> HOURS ON SUNDAY JUNE 13 1652. GREAT POWER
> INSPIRED HIS MESSAGE AND THE MEETING PROVED
> OF FIRST IMPORTANCE IN GATHERING THE SOCIETY
> OF FRIENDS KNOWN AS QUAKERS. MANY MEN AND
> WOMEN CONVINCED OF THE TRUTH ON THIS FELL AND

IN OTHER PARTS OF THE NORTHERN COUNTIES WENT
FORTH THROUGH THE LAND AND OVER THE SEAS WITH
THE LIVING WORD OF THE LORD ENDURING GREAT
HARDSHIPS AND WINNING MULTITUDES TO CHRIST.

Adjacent to the memorial stone is the enclosure of the churchyard, a solitary gravestone and a few stunted trees all that now remains of Firbank chapel destroyed by fire in the nineteenth century. An evocative spot, crowds of Friends still come from far and wide every year close to the anniversary of the 1652 Meeting to join in with the annual open air Worship.

Foxy Faces

Though the numbers of *Vulpes Vulpes* are generally reported as being in a slight decline across the National Park, there are nonetheless two fine and permanent examples of foxes in the Dales, all be it depictions in bronze. The presence of the first of these Reynard reliefs graces the Buckden Pike Memorial Cross, and is associated with the tragic tale of the 'downed' allied aircraft that the memorial commemorates. On 30th January 1942 a Wellington bomber from an allied Polish squadron encountered a severe snowstorm while on a training flight over the Dales and crashed in to the snow covered hillside of Buckden Pike, claiming the lives of all but one of the crew. The surviving injured airman Joseph Fusniak, the plane's rear gunner, managed to drag himself and his badly broken ankle along a trail of snowy fox paw prints

The Fox Head Well at the top of Pateley Bridge High Street

45

hoping they would lead him to habitation, banking on a fox's appetite for domestic fowl. Crawling down Hag Dyke, the prints led him to the village of Cray where he was spotted by the daughter of the landlord of the White Lion. Despite initial suspicions that he was an enemy German pilot in view of Fusniak's limited English, he was well taken care of and made a full recovery. The inclusion of the fox's head on the Buckden Memorial is as a mark of respect for the animal whose paw prints had saved Rear Gunner Fusniak's life.

The second fox features on the aptly named 'Fox's Head Well' in the picturesque Pateley Bridge, the popular and attractive market town nestled in the heart of Nidderdale. Originally erected in 1852 on the Ripon Road and known as the Souter Well, it was moved to the present location at the top of the High Street in the 1870s and became known as the 'Foxes Head Well' because of the bronze water spout in the shape of a fox's head at its centre. With the decline in the demand and necessity for public water supply, invariably the stone trough below the spout today is full to overflowing with a wonderful floral display.

Futuristic Follies, Sorrelsykes, West Burton

The landscape of the Yorkshire Dales is graced with few follies, the functional 'field barn' holding far greater sway in these parts, yet of those fanciful and impractical novelty edifices that still stand, a curious trio harking back to the architectural fashions originating in the eighteenth century still survive in the grounds of Sorrelsykes Park Hall near to West Burton, the charming Dales village where Turner painted a study of the cascading 'Cauldron Falls'.

The Sorrelsykes follies did in fact number four originally, the descriptively named 'Pepper Pot' and 'Rocket Ship' along with a small archway set on the edge of a limestone outcrop dating to the first half of the nineteenth century, and outlasting the fourth folly, the sham facade of a castle with a blank gothic arch which unfortunately blew down in a storm in 1992. Clearly the 1993 grant from the Yorkshire Dales National Park Committee intended to stabilise the follies was sadly too late to save the tumbled down sham castle, yet the remaining three make an unusual and impressive mark on the landscape hereabouts.

G

Gabriel's Ratchetts

Gabriel's Ratchets is the term applied to the regionally specific supernatural pack of flying spectral hounds heard and sometimes seen in the skies over North Yorkshire. These monstrous aerial dogs, also called 'sky yelpers' and sometimes described as possessing human heads were a sure portent of ill-fortune to our forebears. Believed to be hunting the souls of the newly dead, their pack often numbering seven in deference to the number of Cardinal Sins, some even believed them to be the ghosts of unbaptized babies come to hover around the parental home, though sometimes seen by others as spectral birds with glowing eyes that only appeared to those with a relative or friend near death. In 1773 the appearances of these harbingers of misfortune were described by David Naitby, a schoolmaster living in Bedale, in his diary entries for October of that year. With a total of three instances of the Ratchet Pack appearing in the skies over the town, on 18th October he wrote: "*But seven nights now gone since Gabriels raced overhead, and now there has come to us a blood red moon, a sure sign we are to be judged for our sins*".

It has been suggested that the cry of the Ratchets was in fact the sound of flocks of wild geese in flight... In spite of this earthly explanation, the Ratchets were surely a terrifying omen in years gone by.

Gallery On The Green, Settle

A must for connoisseurs of the curious and art lovers alike, the Gallery on the Green, possibly the smallest art gallery in the world, is housed in a converted BT telephone kiosk on The Green in Upper Settle.

Purchased by Settle Town Council in early 2009 under the BT 'Adopt a Kiosk'

Possibly the World's smallest public art gallery – the Gallery On The Green, Settle

47

scheme, once the payphone was removed the Council were free to use the kiosk as they chose. It was agreed that Cultivating Settle, a group dedicated to improving the environment of the town, would manage the facility and set up a 'community art gallery'. While retaining the exterior essence of the iconic K6 type telephone box designed by Sir Giles Gilbert Scott in 1935 to commemorate George V's Silver Jubilee, refurbishment inside and out was funded by a grant obtained from Craven District and Settle Town Councils.

Mounted in what is believed to be the smallest public art gallery in the world, the constantly changing exhibition programme includes works by local, national and international artists. Certainly the Gallery on the Green must be the only gallery filled to capacity with the admission of just two patrons!

Galloper's grave, Giggleswick

In the church of St Alkelda's in Giggleswick village near Settle are the tombs of the Tempest Knights. Hereditary lords of the manor, Sir Richard Tempest (1425-1488) endowed a chantry chapel at Giggleswick and his stone effigy, the figure originally coloured and probably gilt in parts, rests with those of his two (now headless) wives. It is a locally held tradition that Sir Richard was in fact buried along with the head of his favourite war horse, beneath the floor of the Tempest chapel, and during restoration work to the church undertaken between 1890 and 1892 the bones of the Tempest family, knights of an exceptionally tall race, were found mingled with the skull bones of a horse. With only two other confirmed instances of such equine interments uncovered in the north of England, namely at Saxton Church, Sherburn in Elmet (where legend has it that Ranulph Lord Dacre was buried upright on his charger) and at the now ruined Llanercost Priory in Cumbria, the Giggleswick dis-covery was indeed a rare one, and harking back to a far older custom when the interment of a favourite horse, or its head with its late master was a common Celtic burial practice. There is however the head of another four legged representative of the Tempest family present in St Alkelda's, to be found in the carved goat's head acting as the pillow for Sir Richard's effigy. In heraldic terms the goat is emblematic of the victorious martial knight, and pertinent to generations of the Tempest family whose illustrious careers involved battles with the Scots and French as well as

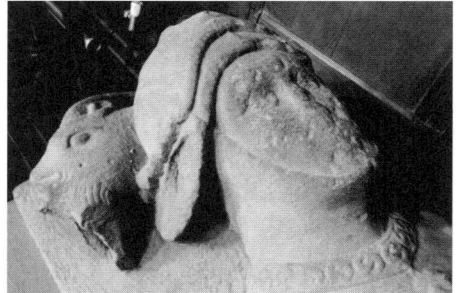

Effigy of Sir Richard Tempest with his head resting on the family emblem

48

in the Wars of the Roses. Sir Richard himself fought at the Battle of Towton, described as probably the largest and bloodiest battle ever fought on English soil. Supporting the House of York he was amongst more than 50,000 soldiers who fought for hours amidst a snowstorm on Palm Sunday, 29th March 1461, shifting the tide of power that displaced the Lancastrian Henry VI in favour Shakespeare's glorious son of York, Edward IV.

Gargoyles that spawned a nursery rhyme, Bolton Priory

Curiously enough, it has been posited that the origins for the nursery rhyme 'Hey Diddle Diddle, The Cat and The Fiddle' are linked to some of the gargoyles adorning the now ruined tower of Bolton Priory. The one time Prior of this once magnificent religious house, named 'Moone' was not entirely bound by his monastic vows, and his less than exemplary antics form the basis for the nursery rhyme – the 'Fiddle' relating to the Prior's unscrupulous misappropriation of church funds – the cow jumping over the moon a coarse reference to his liaison with a local lady, and 'the little dog laughed to see such fun' linked to the one of the gargoyles on the tower of Bolton Priory, a dog which appears to be laughing. One of the other carvings on the Priory tower depicts a pilgrim with what appears to be an alms dish under one arm, and perhaps associated with the last line of the rhyme 'and the dish ran away with the spoon', although another thread to this particular yarn has the Prior's love object running off with the precious church plate! Whether this is the real foundation for the nursery rhyme, the earliest printed version appearing in 1765, the rhyme was almost certainly in circulation long before the lyrics were first written down, and while many other hypotheses have been mooted and there is no concrete historical evidence to support the Moone assumption, if true then it's no wonder the corrupt Prior's ghost is reputed to appear beneath another of the Priory's carvings, that of a roof boss believed to be associated with the Devil himself.

Giant's Grave, West Witton

Not to be confused with its better known namesake at Halton Gill in Upper Wharfedale, the Giant's Grave on the lower slopes of Penhill overshadowing West Witton, the village of 'Burning Bartle' fame – see the letter 'B' for more of this somewhat barbaric ancient custom – is another barrow known as the Giant's Grave. Associated with the terrorizing ogre of folklore said to have had an appetite for flocks of sheep and local maidens alike, his legend is something of a moralising tale, telling how the notoriously brutish Giant inhabiting the heights of Penhill was actually vanquished by his once faithful hound, Wolfhead. One day, with the Giant on the point of devouring an innocent shepherdess, Wolfhead reconsidered his loyalties; chasing his master round and round the hilltop, nipping at his heels, the giant tripped over an inconvenient boulder and pitched head first over Penhill Crags, ending up presumably at the site of the Giant's Grave...

Penhill itself is rich with lore, legend and mystery, and it has been mooted that on the northern facing slopes an ancient hill figure may have existed, forgotten in all but local folklore, but a sound basis for the giant myth nonetheless. As to the somewhat diminutive dimensions of the Giant's Grave, I'll leave the reader to draw their own conclusions...

God's Bridge, Teesdale

Spanning Brow Beck Gill 'God's Bridge' is an impressive natural limestone feature said to be the best example of a 'natural bridge' in Britain. For the geologically curious, the bridge was formed over millennia by the process of sub-riverbed cave development responsible for eroding the rock beneath this Divine span. In times past the bridge was also called 'Trust Bridge', perhaps an allusion to the confidence in those crossing a structure entirely crafted by Nature, though the thousands of walkers annually enjoying the Pennine Way traversing God's Bridge seem confident of the enduring stability of this remarkable feature hewn by the waters still flowing beneath.

Gone Fishing in God's Acre... Ripon Cathedral Graveyard

The tongue-in-cheek wording on one of the the headstones in the graveyard just beyond the east end of Ripon Cathedral attests to the demise of Bryan Tunstall, clearly an enthusiastic fisherman in life:

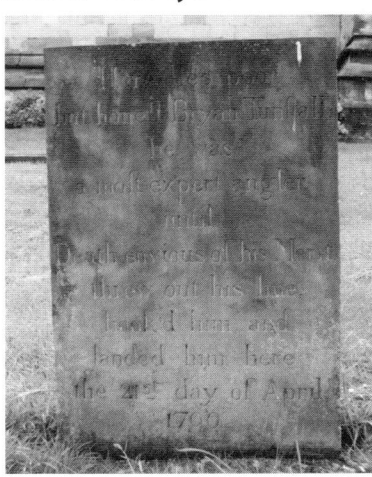

Angling enthusiast Bryan Tunstall's grave, Ripon Cathedral churchyard

> "*Here lies poor,
> but honest Bryan Tunstall,
> he was a most expert angler,
> until Death, envious of his Merit,
> threw out his line,
> hooked him, and
> landed him here
> the 21st day of April 1790.*"

A rather more cheerless yet poetic epithet can be found on the gravestone of John Moore who lies in the churchyard of St

Agatha's in Gilling West, the peaceful Dales village a few miles to the north of Richmond. A victim of highway robbery, Moore was shot from his horse whilst returning from Richmond Market on the 10th of December, 1758. His gravestone is inscribed as follows

> "*Unto the mournful fate of young John Moore,*
> *Who fell a victim to some villain's power,*
> *In Richmond Lane, near to Ask Hall, 'tis said, –*
> *There was his life most cruelly betrayed.*
> *Shot with a gun by some abandoned rake,*
> *Then knock'd o'th' head with a hedging stake,*
> *His soul, I trust, is with the blest above,*
> *There to enjoy eternal rest and love;*
> *Then let us pray his murderer to discover,*
> *That he to justice soon may be brought over.*"

Unfortunately the entreaties of the last two lines never came to pass as according to local records the highwayman 'escaped the hand of justice'.

Gospel Hill Tumulus, Thornton Watlass, near Bedale

A little over half-a-mile to the north of the village of Thornton Watlass is an ancient Early Bronze Age round barrow, known as the *Gospel Hill tumulus*, the name arising from the use of the hill as a venue for early Dissenters to hold their prayer meetings. Toward the end of the seventeenth century, those who did not 'conform' to the governance and usages of the established Church of England separated themselves from the mainstream forms of worship and these 'non-conformists' customarily held their meetings in the open air in adherence to their refusal to enter orthodox places of worship.

As to the original purpose of Gospel Hill, such tumuli or barrows were hemispherical mounds of earth raised over a centralised burial, and in all probability the person entombed within was of considerable social importance: perhaps a tribal chief, a king, a queen, or powerful shaman. In many places across Britain tumuli are often associated with other examples of neolithic monuments in the near vicinity, and Gospel Hill's proximity of the impressive Thornborough Henge is a good example – see the letter ' T' for more details of North Yorkshire's answer to Stonehenge.

Grand Old Duke of York

Perhaps not as old as the nursery rhyme alluded to earlier relating to the gargoyles at Bolton Priory, the 'ten thousand men' boasted of in the eighteenth century nursery rhyme 'The Grand Old Duke of York' were in fact employed in the construction of the hill in the grounds of Allerton Castle, topped with the majestic Temple of Victory.

Allerton Castle, formerly 'Allerton Park', close to the village of Allerton Mauleverer was purchased in 1786 by Prince Frederick, Duke of York, brother to King George IV and a true battlefield royal. According to local legend, the hill on which the Temple of Victory stands, once known as Arbour Hill, is the one mentioned in the nursery rhyme. It was the ant-like activity of workers constantly ascending and descending during the construction of this gigantic mound that inspired the famous nursery rhyme concerning the Grand Old Duke of York and his 10,000 men. Crowned with The Temple of Victory, a fashionable allusion to the ancient Roman temple on the Palatine Hill, this fine octagonal building in the Palladian style is today clearly visible on its 200-foot high hill from the A1 soon after passing the junction for the A59.

The Temple of Victory atop the hill created at the behest of The Grand Old Duke of York

Grewelthorpe Man, the Roman in Kirkby Malzeard churchyard

An unusual interment took place in the churchyard of St Andrews Kirkby Malzeard in 1850 after the body of a well preserved Roman man was discovered in a peat bog on Grewelthorpe Moor. Evidence of Roman occupation had previously been discovered around Kirkby Malzeard, and further attested to when a local workman lost an iron bar down an ancient well whilst extracting stone.

The Grewelthorpe 'bog body' was exposed by two brothers, Edwin and John Grainge of Bramley Grange while cutting peat, and at the time the second only such discovery made in England. Possibly a resident of Romano-British Kirkby, or perhaps an unfortunate lost on the moor and claimed by exposure, more detail can be gleaned from the following extract from the paper written by Thomas C Heslington, presented in 1867 to the Scientific Society of Ripon:

'A few years ago some workmen digging for peat on a farm, on the moors near Kirkby Malzeard, made one of the most extraordinary discoveries, of its nature, ever disclosed. This was the body of a man – evidently an ancient Roman – which the peat had tanned, dried and preserved in a remarkable manner, like (as the people say who saw it) an Egyptian Mummy. The robes were quite perfect and the material tough – having been tanned and preserved by some natural agency. The toga was of a green colour, and some of the dress of scarlet material; the stockings of a yellow cloth, and the sandals cut out in a beautiful shape – like those found in the Thames some years ago – and were likewise finely stitched.'

Somewhere in St Andrew's churchyard at Kirkby Malzeard is the anonymous grave of 'Grewelthorpe Man'

Unfortunately the marvellous state of preservation began to deteriorate immediately on the body's exposure from the covering peat, and virtually destroyed by the time the Kirkby Malzeard policeman arrived, though the local Bobby was astute enough to remove the leggings and sandals from the rapidly decaying corpse. As no coins or weapons were found about the body, it was assumed that he was possibly a wanderer who had lost his way in bad weather and perished on the moor, criss-crossed with ancient tracks between deceptively marshy areas of bog. After some 1400 years immersed beneath the peat Grewelthorpe Man was finally laid to rest in the churchyard of St Andrew's. However, as all the burial records were lost in the fire which destroyed the church in 1908, his place of interment is now unknown. The only tangible reminder of his discovery today is a preserved partial boot, now in the care of York Museum.

H

Hardraw Brass Band Festival, Hardraw, Upper Wensleydale

The tiny village of Hardraw not only boasts what is claimed to be England's highest single-drop water fall – the reputed 100 foot descent to the plunge pool below a popular tourist attraction since the eighteenth century – but is also host to the world famous Hardraw Scar Brass Band Festival, the second oldest outdoor contest of its kind in Britain. Nowadays held annually on the second Sunday in September behind the Green Dragon Inn, the natural amphitheatre surrounding Hardraw Scar waterfall makes this a stunning spot in which to spend a summer Sunday afternoon, listening to some world class competing brass bands play.

The old music contests were started here in 1880 by a committee of public spirited people from and around nearby Hawes who offered substantial prizes (for those days) to the best brass bands and choral societies competing in the grounds of the Scar, lent for the occasion by the Earl of Wharncliffe who was very supportive of the contest. In its heyday the Band Festival drew crowds of many thousands of listeners, with trains bringing people from the manufacturing towns of Yorkshire and Lancashire on a well earned day out. After the contest held in 1883 the famous French tightrope walker Charles Blondin made an appearance and crossed the falls on a high rope at an elevation of 500 feet, cooking an omelette midway! However, after a heavy rain shower rendering the rope difficult to perform on, M. Blondin's celebrated wheelbarrow feat was called off.

Back then the contests were usually held on the last Saturday of June, perhaps to better take advantage of the early summer weather, however on Wednesday 12th July 1899 a tremendous thunderstorm and accompanying cloudburst carved a new watercourse for the Scar, flooding through the Green Dragon Inn and still commemorated by the water level mark in the tap room wall indicating the height of the flood. After this great deluge the contests sadly, for a time, came to an end. That is until after the end of the First World War when Edmund Blythe bought the grounds at Hardraw and laboured intently to revive the renowned brass band contests. Thanks to Mr Blythe's enterprise, a few comparatively local bands were able to hold contests again in the early 1920s, yet despite his efforts and time and money spent to make the revival a success the popularity of Hardraw had by this time waned; the advent of radio meant that music could now be enjoyed inexpensively in the home and by 1927 the contest had finally lapsed. However, nearly 50 years later the event was happily revived in 1976 under the auspices of a group of Kirkby Lonsdale Band members and later the Yorkshire and Humberside Brass Band Association, and in spite of the odd hiatus the event has gone from strength to strength ever since.

Harmonious Hand, Ripon Cathedral

A wonderful curiosity in the form of a carved wooden human hand can be seen protruding from the magnificent organ facing onto the chancel in Ripon Cathedral. The 'Harmonious Hand' is a unique feature that was once used to conduct the choir, operated by a lever on the organ console, an addition to the fine instrument made in 1695 when a rebuild of the organ meant that the organist had to move to a new seat and could no longer see the choir to conduct them himself.

The unique carved wooden hand used to conduct the choir in Ripon Cathedral photographed with the kind permission of the Chapter of Ripon Cathedral

While the first reference to an organ in Ripon Cathedral occurs in the Fabric Rolls for 1399, Ripon Cathedral itself was founded somewhat earlier by St Wilfrid (c. 634-709), who brought craftsmen from the continent to build a new stone church dedicated to St Peter in 672 AD. While the only part of Wilfrid's original church to survive today is the ancient Saxon crypt, Ripon Cathedral in its entirety is truly a treasure.

Hand of Glory, North Stainmore

Of an entirely different ilk to that melodious mitt the Harmonious Hand, a tale comes to us of the one time employment of that prized possession of felons past – the Hand of Glory. To set the scene, during the eighteenth century the isolated Old Spital Inn on Stainmore, situated in country which remains wild even today, was on the centuries old York to Carlisle road (now the A66) a crucial part of the long-distance coaching route, Stainmore the stop where the national mail coach changed horses before heading down the hill in either direction.

Toward the end of the eighteenth century, possibly in 1797, the innkeeper George Alderson was preparing to settle down for the night when a traveller, dressed as a woman, arrived at the inn door begging to stay the night. If she could just rest by the fire – she would be off so early in the morning there was no need that the family should be disturbed by her departure. Not a man to turn away a weary traveller, Alderson admitted the old lady, but asked his servant maid to sit up until the stranger was off the premises.

After Alderson had retired, the maid lay down for a nap on the long settle by the fire but before closing her eyes noticed a pair of men's trousers beneath the old lady's skirts; considering this suspicious she feigned sleep and was right to follow her intuition as, perceiving the maid to be slumbering, the traveller proceeded to take from his bag a 'Hand of Glory' – but before continuing this tale an explanation might be pertinent...

The 'Hand of Glory' was the preserved hand of a hanged man, either the left (the 'sinister' hand) or the hand that had performed the capital offence, and removed from the corpse whilst still on the gallows. Pickled in saltpetre, then dried in the sunshine of the dog days (those sultry days of summer most commonly experienced in the months of July and August), or in an oven with the herb Vervain, candles were then made from the fat of the hanged man, with wicks made from his hair inserted between the fingers. In some cases the whole Hand was dipped in wax and the actual fingers formed the 'candles'. Much coveted by the criminal fraternity the Hand purportedly had the power to unlock any door it came across and to render render motionless all persons to whom it was presented.

Back at the Old Spital Inn, after reciting the magic incantation '*Oh, Hand of Glory, shed thy light, direct us to our spoil tonight*' the disguised old lady went to the inn door to call for his fellow thieves who were concealed outside. The housemaid however, knowing full well the power of the Hand leapt to her feet and bolted the inn door and raised the alarm, yet as she tried to rouse the household all remained sound asleep. Drawing on her remembered folklore she took a jug of milk from the kitchen and extinguished the candle flame, at which point George Alderson immediately woke from his enchanted sleep and fired his blunderbuss towards the thieves. Realising that they were uncovered, the gang said that they would peaceably depart if the Hand were returned to them (clearly a prized object), but Alderson shot at them again and the thieves retreated, leaving the Hand behind – the story goes that the Alderson family kept the Hand of Glory for many years afterwards...

Hart Leap Well, on the old road from Leyburn to Richmond

The small natural spring near the side of the road leading from Richmond to Askrigg over the wide moorland is the Hart Leap Well, and according to local tradition so named as this is the spot celebrated by Wordsworth in his poem of the same name. Legend tells of the chase of a swift and beautiful hart, exhausted after the long pursuit by a lone horseman who had outpaced hounds and fellow huntsmen. Taking three last extraordinary leaps in a bid for freedom, here the hart fell dead by the well, the elements of this tale poignantly woven by Wordsworth into his verse, a monument to the fleeing deer.

Looking out over the expanse of moorland here, this spot, with the sad legend that is attached to it remains as evocative as it must have appeared to Wordsworth in 1799.

Healam Bridge Roman Fort, adjacent to A1 near Pickhill

Sandwiched between the A1 and the newly constructed local access relief road, just north of the turn for Pickhill village is Healam Bridge. Built in 1796, the stone bridge carried the old A1 road over Healam Beck, a crossing place that has existed for centuries as here, adjacent to the busy lanes of traffic, the remains of a second century Roman fort and its associated Vicus were discovered and excavated as part of the £318 million Highways Agency scheme to upgrade the A1 between Dishforth and Leeming.

Centuries old crossing point and the site of a second century Roman fort, the course of the old A1 – Dere Street – was once carried over Healam Bridge. Today the old road terminates with a commemorative stone marking completion of the new carriageway works

Located on Dere Street, the Roman road between Eboracum (York) and Veluniate (Bo'ness) in what is now Scotland, the modern A1 still follows the course of the old road in many places.

Excavations begun in July 2009 unearthed finds which gave archaeologists an invaluable insight into how the local economy supported a Roman military garrison. The remains of a water-powered flour mill used to grind grain and produce food for the soldiers was discovered, as well as food remains, graves and pottery all indicating the presence of a Roman 'industrial estate' sustaining the military presence of the fort and the legions travelling along the Roman road of Dere Street. On a more domestic note, the remarkable discovery of a child's footprints were also uncovered, the configuration of which suggest a boy or girl hopping, skipping or jumping through puddles in the soft ground beside the course of a small stream that ran behind a former Roman vicus settlement.

The archaeological discovery has also generated speculation that the Healam Bridge Fort may have garrisoned the famous Roman Ninth Hispanic Legion – the 'lost legion'. Victorious in campaigns across the Empire, it is believed that the Ninth Legion disappeared after it was sent north to fight the savage Picts in Scotland, never to return...

Highest Pub in Britain

Onwards and upwards, to The Tan Hill Inn which is generally recognised as being the highest pub in England at 1,732feet (528 meters) above sea level. Inevitably the recipient of the first snows of winter before even a flake has fallen on lower levels, the Tan Hill Inn boasts its very own liveried snowmobile, an expedient measure as the possibility of getting snowed in is a very real one. A high point (literally!) on the Pennine Way long distance walk, the Tan Hill Inn is in the heart of real walking country and provides a welcome watering-hole for casual ramblers and ardent walkers alike – as well as host to the ghost of a former publican Mrs Peacock. Mrs Peacock, or Mrs Parrington as she was when she took over the derelict Tan Hill in 1902 with her first husband, ran the isolated

The Tan Hill Inn – where the highest pints in England are pulled!

inn for nearly 40 years, remarrying Michael Peacock after she was left widowed early on with three children. In view of the vulnerability of the inn's isolated position the redoubtable Mrs Peacock took the precaution of keeping a loaded revolver in a handy position just behind the door of the living quarters, often employing the threat of the weapon at closing time to encourage the departure of reluctant customers, and she is known to have fired it at least once. Therefore it comes as no surprise that her spirit still has a vested interest in the place, possibly around closing time!

How Hill Hillfort, Downholme, near Richmond

Best viewed from the convenient lay by on Thorn Hill, the minor road rising from Downholme village on the way to Hudswell, How Hill Fort is a fine example of an Iron Age fortified settlement exploiting the natural elevation of the landscape to defensive advantage, and something of a rarity in North Yorkshire where few such examples exist. Despite the work of the medieval plough (in the Middle Ages the whole of the broad summit of the hill together with the southern and eastern slopes were agriculturally exploited) aerial photography has revealed that the summit was once fully enclosed. Occupying a strategic position How Hill commanded both the Walburn gap, the break in the hills through which leads the route south to the Vale of York, as well as controlling access to upper Swaledale. Possibly later utilised by the Celts until the Roman conquest or even occupied into the post-Roman period, by the time of the Domesday survey in 1086 Downholme had developed into a manor; presumably the inhabitants of How Hill descended from their lofty position to take up life in the lower village.

Hubberholme's Parliament, Upper Wharfedale

While the George Inn in the pretty hamlet of Hubberholme was formerly the local vicarage, today it is very firmly a hostelry. In the days when the Rector was in residence however, Hubberholme being part of the extensive Arncliffe parish, a lighted candle in the window indicated to his flock that the vicar was at home, and to keep up the tradition the pub still keeps a lit candle in the window when the bar is open. Candles are also a vital part of the 'Hubberholme Parliament', a continuing tradition harking back to the eleventh century, with an annual auction still held to let sixteen acres of church land and won by the highest bid made at the moment the candle burns out. The incumbent vicar directs these proceedings from the Inn's dining room, traditionally known as the 'House of Lords', while the auction itself is held in the 'House of Commons', that's the bar of course. A short service is held afterwards at 8pm in the church of St Michael and All Angels, once flooded so badly that fish were seen swimming in the nave, and where a past vicar is said to have carelessly baptised a child *Amorous* instead of *Ambrose*, a mistake that once entered in the parish register couldn't be altered. Perhaps an extended sitting in the 'House of Commons' was to blame? Regardless of this baptismal error, 'Amorous' Stanley used his memorable name to his advantage later in life when he became a hawker.

Hunter's Stone, North Moor, Coverdale

Just half a mile from Tor Dyke, the linear earthwork crossing the valley head guarding access from Upper Wharfedale into Coverdale, on the lonely road crossing North Moor heading for Horsehouse is the Hunter's Stone. Set by the roadside in the shadow of Great Whernside, usually the first recipient of the early winter's snows, this nearly seven foot tall guidestone made from sandstone marks the once important route used by monks and drovers connecting Kettlewell with Coverham Abbey. Incised with a small cross on one face, now incredibly worn with the ravages of time and the elements, the Hunter's Stone is said to perform an unusual party piece – when the clock at

The Hunter's Stone on lonely North Moor, Coverdale

nearby Hunter's Hall (now re-named Coverhead Farm) strikes midnight the Hunter's Stone spins around. North Moor is a truly breathtakingly desolate landscape, though a popular stopping point for those wishing to take advantage of the footpaths criss-crossing the moor up Whernside and dropping down into Kettlewell. The moor is also dotted with the burial mounds of fallen Brigantes tribesman who were on the losing side when the Roman Empire held sway in these parts - for more of the restless spirits of slain warriors said to still haunt their old battle ground see the entry for 'Tor Dyke' under the letter 'T'.

Hutton Monument, Marske, near Richmond
Visible from the Marske to Fremington road, in the parkland surrounding Marske Hall is the Hutton Monument. This sandstone ashlar obelisk standing at just under one thousand feet tall was erected to commemorate Sir Matthew Hutton of Macclesfield, brother of the then owner, who died 12th December 1814 aged 35 years. In accordance with Sir Matthew's particular request he was buried on the spot now marked by the obelisk as it was here, when a boy, he had often sat to enjoy his favourite views of the family estate and surrounding imposing landscape.

Other members of the Hutton family rest in the more traditional environs of St Edmund's Church, the patronage of which has been in the Hutton family since 1598 when Matthew Hutton, Archbishop of York purchased the estate. The Hutton's of Marske are the only family in the United Kingdom who can be said to have yielded to the Church of England two archbishops, and within two centuries of each other. The first Matthew Hutton becoming Archbishop of York in 1595, and a later Matthew created Archbishop of York in 1747 and of Canterbury in 1757.

I

Ibby Peril, River Dee, Dentdale

Shown on current Ordnance Survey maps as 'Ibbeth Peril' this curiously named waterfall draws on the legend of the ghost of a witch named 'Ibby Peril', one time resident of Dent, but now doomed to eternally frequent a secret dark cave concealed behind the falls. A feared and sinister old crone who lured drunken locals into her clutches as they passed by in the pitch dark of night, it is said said that most were taken into the foreboding chamber of her cave, beneath the fall, where she concocted her spells and dark magic. If they were lucky Ibby might leave them to sleep off their hangovers, the less fortunate were drowned in the plunge pool.

Ibby got a mention in Harry Speight's *Craven and the North West Yorkshire Highlands* published in 1892, with the warning that this watery wraith lay in wait to snare any unsuspecting soul who ventured too close. However these days Ibby is far more likely to snag a passing canoeist as the series of waterfalls on this section of the River Dee prove an active challenge.

A further demonic watery association in the vicinity can be found about half a mile upstream from the perilous falls in the evocatively named Hell's Cauldron. After the Dee passes beneath Tommy Bridge and over the water-worn pavements of limestone, after flowing through a deep ravine the river cascades into a dark plunge

Ibbeth Peril in calm mood, and no sign of the witch...

pool beneath the dense tree canopy. After spells of heavy rainfall both Ibbeth Peril and Hell's Cauldron can be a fearsome sight, though still worth a visit even in clement conditions.

Ice Houses

While the North Yorkshire climate isn't noted for its torrid summers, nevertheless in the days before modern refrigeration many country estate houses would have made good use of an Ice House. Generally this would be a brick-lined pit sunk into the ground with a domed roof to control the circulation of air. Often sited under trees and some way from the house, within the structure would be some form of drainage at the bottom with the ice packed between layers of straw, having been cut from nearby ponds or lakes in wintertime; ice would then be available throughout the year. Because they were tucked away and vegetation was encouraged to grow over them, the presence of ice houses isn't always obvious, however there are some interesting examples still extant in the Dales, and one such can be spied in the private walled garden of the Georgian Old Vicarage in Pickhill, near Thirsk. Another still graces the grounds of Constable Burton Hall, the handsome Palladian villa standing at the entrance to Wensleydale, and the the aptly named Ice House Wood on the outskirts of Knaresborough is so named as here an ice house once stood that supplied nearby Scriven Hall, sadly destroyed by fire in 1954.

Ilkley Moor Alien Sighting

In 1978, while out walking on Ilkley Moor, retired police officer Philip Spencer spotted and managed to photograph what he thought was an alien being. Adding fuel to Ilkley Moor's already mysterious and intriguing reputation as an extra terrestrial hot-spot, though the image was somewhat blurry, to many the sighting lent weight to the numerous reports of alien activity witnessed in the area. Although the proximity of Leeds Bradford Airport and RAF Menwith Hill have been mooted as possible explanations for the claimed UFO sightings and odd lights seen through the mists of Ilkley Moor, the erratic behaviour of Philip Spencer's compass and the 'lost time' affecting his wrist watch are nonetheless perturbing aspects factored into the account of his encounter...

A more down to earth explanation however can be given for what appears to be a 'spaceship' visible above Arnagill Crags in Colsterdale. This edifice is in fact a sighting tower, one of a series of four known as the Colsterdale Towers, and used to conduct surveys during the construction of the Roundhill and Leighton Reservoirs built by the Harrogate Water Corporation between 1895 and 1911, and not an extraterrestrial conveyance!

Ilton's Stonehenge, near Masham

You might think it odd to find a scaled down version Stonehenge in the woods just three miles from the market town of Masham, however this isn't a consequence of the architects of Salisbury Plain come to the Yorkshire Dales, but the brainchild of William Danby, former owner of Swinton Park. Danby almost entirely rebuilt his family seat at Swinton in the early 1800s, and took the altruistic opportunity of making a 'gothic' landscape addition to the country park using local labour in a bid to ease the prevalent unemployment in the area. Hence the Druid's Temple was constructed by local workers who were paid a shilling a day to build this labour intensive folly, the enormous stone altars, menhirs, dolmens and sarsens standing firm today within Forestry Commission land, and a popular spot with picnickers.

William Danby also offered a further pecuniary reward which was succinctly described in a guide to the district dated 1910 and ran thus "*the*

Set in wonderful wooded surroundings, the Druid's Temple – the imaginative man-made folly commissioned in the 1820s for the Swinton Park Estate in a bid to ease local economic hardship

builder of the temple offered to provide any individual with food, and a subsequent annuity, providing he would reside in the temple seven years, living the primitive life, speaking to no one and allowing his beard and hair to grow." It is said that one man accepted the challenge, lasting four and a half years, at the end of which he was compelled to admit defeat. Apparently no other would-be hermits were tempted by William Danby's generous whimsy...

Indian's Turban, Brimham Rocks, near Pateley Bridge

Just one of the curious rock formations to be found at Brimham Rocks in Nidderdale where fifty acres of Millstone Grit outcrops have been carved into strange shapes by the erosion of wind and rain over millennia. The much loved and much visited Rocks are now in the care of the National Trust and present something of a geological playground, with uninhibited access for those wanting to enjoy fresh air and the splendid views out across Nidderdale. As well as the Indian's Turban, Brimham boasts many other imaginatively named outcrops such as the Dancing Bear, the Druid's Writing Desk, the Sphinx, the Watchdog, the Camel, the Turtle and even a Baboon amongst others.

A flavour of the strange and wonderful rock formations at Brimham

Itinerant Saint seeks cave in Knaresborough area

Saint Robert of Knaresborough, whose feast day falls on 24th September, though never officially canonised is still considered as one of the outstanding saints of the early thirteenth century with churches dedicated to him both at Knaresborough and Pannal in North Yorkshire. Of privileged birth, Robert Flower (alternatively spelt Floure or Fleur) was the son of Touk Flower, Mayor of York in 1160. Very early in his life Robert joined the monastic order of the Cistercians, but remained only a few months as he thought he could better serve God through seeking a life of solitude.

Though Robert's cave at Knaresborough is the location venerated as the saint's hermitage, he was forced to move several times. Having to share his first cave near Grimhall Bridge with a knight who was in hiding from a wrathful King Richard I, after the monarch's death the knight returned home leaving

Robert in the solitude he craved. Some years later a wealthy widow offered Robert tenure in a cell at St Hilda's Chapel in Rudfarlington not far from his original cave, and here he developed a reputation as a wise and holy man, caring for the poor.

However, just a year after moving to St Hilda's, Robert's hermitage was destroyed by bandits and he was forced to live in the lee of the church wall at Spofforth for a while, before attempting to live with the monks at Hedley Priory, near Tadcaster. This new arrangement was short lived however as Robert found the Benedictine style of monastic life far too lax, and he returned to the now bandit free Rudfarlington.

Well known for his charity to the poor and destitute, Robert often worked to free men from prison; this however resulted in him falling foul of the authorities who, accusing him of harbouring thieves and outlaws, destroyed the St Hilda's hermitage for a second time, forcing Robert to move back to his original cave in Knaresborough where he stayed for the rest of his life.

Towards the end of his days, pilgrims flocked to Robert seeking spiritual guidance and asking to be healed of physical ailments, they even continued to come to the cave in large numbers for centuries after his death in 1218. Robert's brother Walter, following in their father's footsteps was then Mayor of York, and paid for some new buildings in the vicinity of the cave, including a chapel dedicated to the Holy Cross. Today visitors continue to visit the saint's cave, carved into the face of the limestone cliff, and the remains of the chapel.

J

Jacobite graves, Low Row, Swaledale

In the churchyard of Holy Trinity, serving the adjoining settlements of Feetham and Low Row that stretch along the main road through the lovely Swaledale, are buried the remains of several Jacobite rebels.

Discovered during construction of the Parsonage in 1846, the human skeletons were interred in a mound closeby and had apparently been buried in military clothing, as the buckle of a sword belt and other small item were found with the bones. Tradition holds that a skirmish occurred somewhere in the neighbourhood between the locals and the Scots of the Young Pretender's army and the 'Dalesmen,' and it was supposed that these were the remains of seven of the former who had fallen in the encounter. These rebel supporters of Charles Edward Stuart's attempt to regain the British throne now lay amongst the other graves, overlooking this magnificent and wild Dales landscape.

Janet's Foss, Gordale Scar, Malhamdale

In the Old Norse language *Foss* is the word for waterfall, and Janet (or Jennet as she is sometimes known) was supposedly the fairy queen who held sway in the district, living in a cave behind the falls.

Carved by the waters of the melting glaciers, the dramatic limestone gorge of Gordale Scar is today filled by the flowing waters of the Gordale Beck. As the stream leaves the gorge tumbling over the moss covered limestone outcrop of Janet's Foss, the falls drop into the deep pool below. Nestled in a magical wood and reached by

Does the Fairy Queen still dwell behind Janet's Foss?

the footpath from Malham Village, Janet's Foss inspired both Wordsworth's pen and Turner's brush alike, and it is easy to imagine that Janet and her retinue still inhabit this enchanting location.

Jangling Annas

Kirkby Stephen in the former old county of Westmorland is a traditional market town remote from larger populations, and the Monday livestock market still held in the market square dating back to the town's original charter granted in 1352 is still an important event in the town and surrounding countryside. Kirkby Stephen boasts many historic buildings and structures, and Franks' Bridge, the seventeenth century corpse lane bridge supposedly named for one Francis Birbeck, a local brewer, still retains a coffin stone where the dead could be rested on their way to burial from the nearby hamlets of Hartley and Winton. It was said for centuries that the bridge was also haunted, by a noisy ghost known as 'Jangling Annas'. Making his presence known with the jangling sound of his chained wrists, Annas was an escaped prisoner from nearby Hartley Castle, thirteenth century home to Sir Andrew de Harcala (today only a fragment of the medieval castle wall remains in a farmyard). Jangling or 'Jingling' Annas as he is otherwise known, drowned in the river beneath Frank's Bridge, probably inhibited from doing the breaststroke as his hands were supposed to have been reduced to stumps by the manacles he was forced to wear during his confinement.

Frank's Bridge, Kirkby Stephen, said to be the noisy haunt of 'Jangling Annas'

Apparently Jingling Annas used to cause travellers a great deal of trouble and eventually had to be dealt with. The story goes that the spirit of Jingling Annas was finally laid to rest under a rock, near the bridge, by the Wise Man of Stainmore, a local shamen with the abilities to lay 'dobbies' and other restless spirits. Were Annas still active today however, he'd have have to increase the volume of his jangling chains to be heard over the noisy population of Macaws flying freely around the town, their loud squawking and occasional chatter a surprising and colourful feature of daily life in Kirkby Stephen when these beautiful birds are not at home in the refuge set up for unwanted parrots on the outskirts of town.

Jenny Green Teeth

A well known figure in Dales folklore said to inhabit lakes, pools and rivers, Jenny Green Teeth is a water spirit with a malevolent reputation, though she may have been the invention of concerned parents through the ages in a bid to protect children from the dangers of drowning...

Tales of her existence are embellished by her hideous appearance, Jenny's skin entirely green as is her long weed like hair, and with large saucer eyes and razor-sharp teeth she likes nothing better than to prey on small children as their flesh is tender and tastier, dragging beneath the surface any foolish child who gets too close to the water's edge.

There is one particularly graphic tale of the watery demise of a young boy who failed to heed his grandmother's warnings about Jenny Greenteeth. Though it was winter time and food was scarce, the grandmother was adamant that the boy should not attempt to catch fish from the river. Ignoring her entreaties he fell victim to the rumble in his belly and Jenny's wet clutches. On seeing a fish tangled in some algae, as he reached into the water he noticed that the green weed was in fact spreading up his arms. Recoiling in fright the boy realised the algae was actually a pair of long green arms with hideous gnarled talon-like fingernails, but it was too late; Jenny's grinning face beneath the surface was the last thing the boy saw before he was pulled under and drowned.

Also known as *Ginny Green Teeth*, *Wicked Jenny* or *Nell-o'* or *Peg-o'-the-Well*, her favourite haunts are the River Ribble and the Tees, though at the latter she is known locally as Peg Prowler, and renowned here for her demands that a living sacrifice be made every seven years, in the absence of which she takes matters into her own hands and snatches a human for herself. Also active further downstream where the Ribble flows west into Lancashire, at Brungerley stepping stones Jenny is said to similarly exact the toll of a human life every seven years, claimed by grabbing some unsuspecting traveller and pulling him beneath the water to drown; clearly this is a spot imbued with misfortune as it was while attempting to cross these stepping stones that the hapless and recently defeated King Henry VI was captured after the Battle of Hexham in 1464, later deposed and murdered in the Tower of London.

Incidentally the nicknames applied to Jenny are sometimes used to identify a type of aquatic plant, otherwise called duckweed that grows and covers the entire surface of ponds and pools, giving the appearance of an even, grassy expanse and making it very dangerous, especially for children.

Jenny Twigg and her Daughter Tib, Fountains Earth Moor, near Pateley Bridge

On the remote bog scattered moorland, part of the broad expanse of Fountains Earth Moor, stand the twin towering stone stacks of Jenny Twig and her daughter Tib, distinct from the neighbouring millstone grit outcrop of Sypeland Crags. In 1863, William Graing rather romantically referred to the pair as '*Giantesses in broad bonnetts*', however local lore conjures a rather more siniter image of the pair, the Twig mother and daughter who have stood side by side for millennia associated with murder. Said to have been responsible for the demise of the three Scottish pedlars whose headless bodies were found in a shallow grave on the summit of Dead Man's Hill – see their entry under the letter 'D' – though nothing could be proven, legend has the wicked mother and daughter rock combo turned to stone as punishment for their misdoings, millennia of harsh elements having shaped these pillars of millstone grit into forms resembling contorted human faces.

The origins of an old local rhyme are also said to been rooted in the tales of the evil mother and daughter, immortalised in the uncanny rock features:

> '*Jenny Twigg, Jenny Twigg*
> *Jenny Twigg and her daughter Tib,*
> *Jenny Twgg, Jenny Twigg,*
> *Jenny Twigg and her black cat Gibbe*'

Jew Stone, Outhgill

Though the homesteads of Outhgill are few and isolated, they actually comprise to make this small community the main hamlet in the sparsely populated dale of Mallerstang. Retaining the Norse pattern of the original settlement, the inn, post office and smithy of the nineteenth century have long since closed, and the only bygone survivors are the fourteenth century church of St Mary and the 'Jew Stone' set on the village green, though technically the latter is a replica of the original monument set up in 1850.

The Jew Stone commemorates eccentric William Mounsey's walk from the mouth of the River Eden on the Solway Marshes to the river's source on Black Fell Moss near Outhgill, Mounsey arriving there on the Ides of March 1850. Often referred to as 'the Carlisle Jew' Mouncey was a solicitor of that town, and though not Jewish earned the soubriquet as he habitually dressed in the style of an Orthodox Jew and wore his beard long. However there is another theory as to how the Jew Stone got its named, and supposedly the reason for the original monument's destruction. Carved with an inscription in Latin and Greek, in 1870 a group of navvies working on the Settle-Carlisle Railway line found the stone and unable to understand the mystical writing thought it the work of the Devil and promptly smashed it to pieces!

Fast forward to World War II when a polish artilleryman named Shalom Herman found a reference to the stone on a map he was using during training at Warcop camp. Another forty years passed, yet the Jew Stone obviously stuck in Herman's memory. Now an Israeli minister he returned to the UK to look for the stone and on finding it still broken, the fragments of Dent marble in an impossible state of repair, he instigated fund raising in Cumbria and Israel in order to have a replica made. The new Jew Stone, an exact copy carved from a more durable limestone, was erected in Outhgill in 1989 in memory of William Mouncey, and the inscription, still in Latin and Greek, translates as:

'The stone was smashed by navvies from the Settle and Carlisle Railway, who couldn't read it, 1870. The pieces were rescued about the late 1940s, but couldn't be restored. This exact replica is made of a better limestone.'

Jingle Pot, Chapel-le-Dale

The curiously named Jingle Pot is one of a series of three 'pots', the others named the Hurtle Pot and Alum Pot, where the water filled subterranean limestone passages of Chapel Beck's flooded cave system open to the surface.

A favourite with cave divers, this trio of pots can be found near the hamlet of Chapel-le-Dale, nestled between Ingleborough and Whernside. These virtual 'windows' into Chapel Beck's flooded cave system were one of the subjects sketched by the romantic landscape painter Turner during his many tours of North Yorkshire, inspired by the spirituality he found in the glorious landscapes, Turner returned repeatedly to the Dales to capture the beauty he found.

As to the Jingle Pot's name, this is said to derive from the the strange jingling, rattling sound made by stones when thrown into its recesses, though during

The mysterious 'throbbing' Hurtle Pot, along with the Jingle and Alum Pots makes up the trio of water filled entrances to the subterranean Chapel-le-Dale cave system

times of flood the peculiarly hollow jangling sound is inaudible as the water 'boils' out of this hole, similar to the conditions producing the curious rhythmic throbbing sound periodically pulsing up from the subterranean depths of the Hurtle Pot. Though the rush of water through the cave system after heavy rainfall is the more likely and earthly explanation for the pounding noise, legend lays the blame on the resident ghost said to live in the Hurtle Pot, who is also blamed for the deaths of any unfortunates drowned in the depths of his watery haunt.

Julius Caesar buried in Masham?!

Well not the Roman Imperial Emperor... rather the eighteenth century landscape and watercolour painter Julius Caesar Ibbetson. His imperious forenames were given as a direct result of his caesarean delivery, his mother going into premature labour as a result of a fatal fall on ice, and to Ibbetson a lifelong source of embarrassment.

A native of Leeds, apprenticed as a ship painter and later working as a picture restorer, Ibbetson developed a thorough appreciation of the works and methods of the Dutch artists and in 1785 himself exhibited at the Royal Academy.

After a series of personal disasters beginning with the death of his first wife, serious illness and severe financial difficulties, in 1803 Ibbetson met the Yorkshire landowner and philanthropist William Danby, and by 1805 had moved to Masham as Danby's protégé. Here, surrounded by his young family and a welcoming community, he spent the only settled period of his life reflected in some of the prolific charming local scenes he

Julius Caesar Ibbetson's grave, St Mary's churchyard, Masham

captured, including a study of his mentor in a fashionably sporting pose with hunting dog and gun, and his oil *Market Day, Masham* painted in 1811. Ibbetson died on 13 October 1817 and was buried in the churchyard of St Mary's in Masham, an evocative view of which he had painted from across the River Ure.

K

Katherine Parr's Oak, Thorpe Perrow, near Bedale

Katherine Parr's Oak, Thorpe Perrow Arboretum

Holding the distinction of having been Henry VIII's sixth and last wife, at the time of Katherine's unlooked for wedding to the increasingly overweight, tyrannical and much married king, she had herself been widowed for the second time. Katherine and her late husband John Neville, 3rd Lord Latimer resided at Snape Castle, located in the village of the same name close to Bedale, and adjoining the beautifully laid out arboretum at Thorpe Perrow. Amongst the eighty five acres of parkland famed as one of the finest private collections of trees and shrubs in the country, of the many impressive specimens one from the sizteenth century still flourishes, the romantically named 'Katherine Parr's Oak'. This resplendent old tree having shed its acorns for hundreds of years was probably attributed to Henry's sixth queen in view of the tree's proximity to her former home; perhaps a more transient reminder of Katherine Parr's presence is the ghost of a Blue Lady said to still haunt the environs of Snape Castle, her countenance radiating serenity and calm.

Kelpies, Cover Bridge, Lower Wensleydale

If you decide to take advantage of the warming fire side welcome and local ales on offer at the Cover Bridge Inn (and have managed to negotiate the unusual door latches that are an original feature of the pub), you might well notice the carved stone bust of a strange horse-like creature in one of the alcoves in the public bar. This is a representation of a Kelpie, a supernatural 'water horse' that dates back thousands of years to Celtic folklore. There are numerous stories and legends associated with this mythical creature, whose traditional haunts usually favour the rivers and lakes of Scotland and Ireland, however those that inhabit the watery environs of Cover Bridge are the rarest of breeds as their presence in the North of England is very unusual; rising from the foaming waters at the confluence of the rivers Cover and Ure at dusk, they stalk their victims before pursuing them to a watery demise!

The Inn at Cover Bridge itself can lay claim to an age-old heritage. Situated between the two bridges over the River Ure and the River Cover, at this point the ancient road from Richmond and the North crossed the Ure then continued up Coverdale. As an old coaching inn it was called the Forresters Arms, before that the Masons Arms, but there has been an inn on the site for well over 400 years, as in 1536 the last Abbot of Jervaulx Abbey entrusted the landlord with the secret recipe for Wensleydale Cheese, famously produced by the brothers at Jervaulx before the abbey was decimated by the Reformation and Abbot Sedbar executed for his part in the ill fated Pilgrimage of Grace.

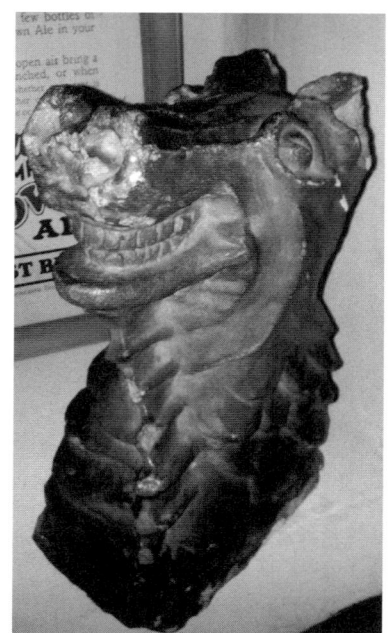

Carved bust of the Cover Bridge Kelpie

This truly is a lovely spot for a pint or two, but if you fancy an evening stroll along the delightful riverside path that follows the River Cover as it flows through the steep-sided wooded gorge known as Cover Banks, just remember to decline any offer of an aquatic horseback ride!

Kilnsey Crag, Kilnsey, Wharfedale

The iconic and imposing limestone cliff of Kilnsey Crag is an unmissable natural feature on the road between Kettlewell and Grassington. Standing around 170 feet high with an overhang of 40 feet, Kilnsey Crag is a real climbing hotspot.

Created by the Wharfedale glacier during the last Ice Age, Turner visited Kilnsey Crag on his tour of Yorkshire in 1816; he spent the night of 25th July at nearby Kettlewell and devoted the next morning to exploring Kilnsey Crag, making various sketches and a watercolour study from the south of the Crag. However, it is not noted whether or not he encountered the spirit of 'Old Nan', the locally renowned witch who once lived beneath the overhang of Kilnsey

Crag in the 1700s. Old Nan, whose real name was Nancy Winter was famous throughout the Craven district for telling people's fortunes, and had a witchcraft shop in Bag's Alley in Skipton. How effective her predictions were remains questionable in view of the fact that '*her stock of spells was not very large*', Old Nan relying on her pet guinea pig and half a pack of dirty playing cards in divining futures!

Kingsley's inspiration for *The Water-Babies*, Malham Tarn, Malhamdale

It was in 1858, while visiting his friend Walter Morrison at High Trenhouse which overlooks the tranquil glacial lake of Malham Tarn, that author Charles Kingsley was inspired to write his novel the *The Water-Babies*. Malhamdale was to prove a draw for many influential visitors in the Victorian era, Morrison counting John Ruskin and Charles Darwin amongst his house guests. The remote, upland estate at Malham Tarn was a good six or eight mile walk from the nearest railway stations at Bell Busk or Settle, and though it was well known that Morrison himself preferred to make the journey on foot to his 'mountain home', there would doubtless have been a horse and carriage awaiting his guests. On such a journey Kingsley would have travelled up the steeply winding road of Cove Lane, affording his first glimpse of the white cleanliness of the limestone countryside of Malham Cove where the dark smudges on the limestone reminded him of the soot left behind by the 'climbing boys' as they swarmed up and down chimney walls, and where the sparkling clear water of the River Aire flowed from the base of the cliff, creative components for the story of *The Water Babies*, subtitled by Kingsley as *A Fairy Tale for a Land Baby*.

Malham Cove
(Painted by late nineteenth century landscape artist Arthur Streeton)

Kirk Carrion, Lunedale Ridge, near Middleton in Teesdale

A solitary stand of mature Scots pines on the Lunedale Ridge some ten miles to the north-west of Barnard Castle mark the site of one of the region's major Bronze Age burial mounds. The tumulus known as Kirk Carrion is thought to

Silhouetted against the skyline, the tumulus of Kirk Carrion dominating the Lunedale Ridge

be the tomb of the Brigantine prince Caryn hence the name 'Kirkcarrion' meaning Caryn's Castle, and constructed some time around 1400 BC. In 1804 the site was excavated and the disturbance of the cinerary urn and bones found therein gave rise to the local legends and ghost stories attached to this spot. It is said that no matter how rough the weather, within the circle of trees atop the ridge the wind never blows, and when the full moon is up the unsettled spirit of Caryn stalks the ridge, angry at the desecration of his Celtic resting place. Whatever the truth behind these myths, Kirkcarrion is certainly an atmospheric place. A chieftain's tomb where the wind never blows...

Kisdon Force Waterfall, near Keld, Swaledale

Kisdon Force is a picturesque waterfall beneath Kisdon Hill, a short distance downstream from the village of Keld in Swaledale. While today the falls are admired by walkers making a detour from the popular Pennine Way, in the seventeenth century Kisdon Force was the venue for clandestine meetings of non-conformists who, before the first Presbyterian chapel in Swaledale was built in 1690 would hold secret services behind the the waterfall. While the faithful congregated in this unconventional place of worship, one member of their group would be posted as a look-out, and possibly accounting for reports from some visitors of an eerie sensation of of being watched...

Knights Templar Preceptory, Penhill, Wensleydale

In a field besides the road running from West Witton to Swinithwaite are the ruins of a preceptory of the Knights Templar, founded by Roger Mowbray around the year 1200. The Templars, along with their arch rivals the Hospitallers, or Knights of St John, were a military order of fighting monks founded in the twelfth century to better protect pilgrims travelling to Jerusalem. Originating in Outremer, 'The Land beyond the Sea', which was the medieval name for the Holy Land at the time of the Crusades, according to tradition their headquarters were built on the site of the ancient Temple of Solomon, and hence how the order derived its name.

First introduced to Britain in 1146 the Order were essentially a secret society, the Templars ruled over by a Grand Master, and their mysterious rites and ceremonies known only to initiates of the brotherhood. While the covert nature of the order created a tightly knit brotherhood, this also laid the Templars open to the accusations of those keen to destroy the increasingly powerful, wealthy and arrogant Knights whose influence had grown from their traditional stomping grounds in Palestine to the political arenas of medieval Europe.

Accusations of heresy and witchcraft led to arrests and 'confessions' extracted by torture, with the origins of the 'Friday 13th' superstition harking back to the initial arrests made at dawn on Friday 13th October 1307; over the succeeding seven years, hundreds of Templars were burnt at the stake, their assets confiscated and the Order decimated. As a consequence the Penhill Preceptory was dissolved in 1308-12 and passed to the Knights Hospitallers, though by 1328 they accounted it worthless due to its ruinous state. And so it remained. Excavated in 1840, the foundations of the stone built chapel were uncovered along with three stone coffins with cover slabs and in the chancel the stone base of an altar, which still shows through the turf today.

Remains of the Kinights Templar Preceptory, Penhill, Wensleydale

L

Lacon Cross, Lacon Hill, near Sawley Village
This stone cross base and partial shaft is a vestige of the days when Fountains Abbey possessed a number of outlying granges from which the Cistercian brothers co-ordinated agricultural and industrial work, harnessing from the landscape the raw materials for the monastery's subsistence; food, clothing, utensils and building materials. Traversing a network of tracks and lanes to these outlying communities, in bad weather such boundary crosses were invaluable indicators to travellers that they were on the right road. Standing in a field near Lacon Hall, close to the village of Sawley, this surviving boundary cross marked the road from Fountains' grange at Warsill to the abbey precinct via Butturton Bridge, another example of the monks thirteenth century networking endeavours, the impressive stone span providing access to the abbey estates.

Lady Algitha's Cave, near Leyburn
The opening to this secret cave discovered in the late 19th Century lays in Warren Wood beneath the scar along which runs the Leyburn Shawl – the curiously named footpath on the escarpment leading from Leyburn town warranting its own entry under the letter 'L'. About 20 feet deep, the cave yielded finds of animal bones and human remains, as well as potsherds and a hearth suggesting a Neolithic presence in this part of Wensleydale some ten thousand years ago.

Given the dating of the cave's discovery, the name may commemorate Lady Algitha Lumley who married into the Orde-Powlett family in 1868, hereditary barons of nearby Bolton Castle, the cave finds given over to the care of the castle museum.

Lady Hill, Aysgarth
Rising from the far side of the River Ure, the glacial landform of Lady Hill is a well known landmark seen from the road between Aysgarth and the tiny hamlet of Worton. A heavy dose of Faerie folklore is attached to the hill, as memory holds as far back as the twelfth century when four unlucky people were abducted from Aysgarth by the faerie folk supposedly inhabiting Lady Hill...

Home of the faeries? A wintery view of Lady Hill blanketed in snow

17th Century map of Mallerstang showing Hugh Seat – the hill bottom right of centre marked as 'Huseat Morvel hill'. Also shown are Pendragon Castle and the archaically spelt 'Kirkby Steuen', both on the Lady Anne's Way

There is also a local legend that Lady Hill was named for the ill-fated Mary Queen of Scots, imprisoned for a spell at Nappa Hall, the fortified manor house less than three miles away as the crow flies and with an uninterrupted view of Lady Hill. While the Scots Queen was held at Nappa as a respite from her confinement within the walls of Bolton Castle, she may well have enjoyed the vista. It is said that her wraith haunts Nappa Hall, attired in black velvet, heading for the winding stone staircase in the direction of the west tower, perhaps drawn by the view...

Lady's Pillar, Hugh Seat, Mallerstang

On the summit of Hugh Seat, the fell in Mallerstang lying on the present border between Cumbria and the Yorkshire Dales National Park, stands a stone pillar erected in 1664 at the behest of Lady Anne Clifford. Closely associated with Lady Anne, this dale at the head of the upper Eden Valley is indelibly marked with her efforts to help repair the damage caused to the area by long years of border wars and raids, and the upheavals of the English Civil War. Castles, churches and almshouses benefited from her restoring efforts, and the ancient road to the east of the River Eden is known as 'Lady Anne's Way' in memory of the indomitable Countess of Pembroke who often travelled along this track while moving between her many residences. As for the pillar that bears her name, this commemorates one of her predecessors, Sir Hugh de Morville, Lord of the manor of Mallerstang in the late twelfth century and one of the four knights who murdered St Thomas Becket in Canterbury Cathedral on 29th December 1170. Legend holds that de Morville sought refuge at his northern manor before his banishment to France – Hugh Seat is named after him – and that his penitent thoughts were haunted by the view of Wild Boar Fell as the outline of this highest point of Mallerstange Edge, in certain lights, bears an uncanny resemblance to the face and mitre of the murdered archbishop.

Lammerside Castle, near Kirkby Stephen

In sight of the Settle-Carlisle Railway, on the beautiful west side of Wharton Fell are the ruins of Lammerside Castle, a few hundred yards from the bend in the River Eden as it passes through the valley and on towards Pendragon Castle, mentioned later under the letter 'U'. Dating to sometime in the 1300s the tower and now vanished attendant buildings may have been built by the Warcops, with a branch of the Wharton family later occupying it until the late 1400s. Functioning as a Pele Tower, Lammerside with its strengthened central keep was one of a series of small fortified tower houses built along the English and Scottish borders, intended as watch towers and a place of refuge from the marauding Scots and Border Reivers once destructively active in the vicinity.

Leech House, Bedale

Claimed to have been the most common medical practice performed by surgeons from antiquity until the late 19th century, for nearly 2,000 years the leech has been raised specifically for medical use. Famed as a cure-all, it was believed that through bloodletting, a standard treatment for almost every ailment, leeches would drain 'impure blood' from the body, thereby alleviating illness. Supplied by apothecaries to be administered to patients suffering anything from a gumboil to persistent headaches, a ready supply of leeches was essential and in Bedale we find a small red brick building close to the Bedale Beck, believed to be the only surviving Leech House in the country. The Grade II Listed building dating back to the eighteenth century was used to store leeches, kept alive with the

Bedale Leech House

fresh water flowing from the adjacent beck, until such times as doctors requested them for treatment, the local apothecary collecting the specified number of leeches and delivering them in a special jar. Though 'leeching' may seem a gruesome treatment, the potential for the effective use of leeches has been recognised by modern medicine, and today these slimy parasites are effectively employed in plastic and reconstructive surgery procedures, the natural anticoagulant secreted from their bite immensely beneficial in preventing clots and restoring proper blood flow.

Although the Bedale Leech House can only be viewed on special heritage open days – a word to the squeamish – there are no longer any leeches in residence!

Leper Hospital, Ripon

The tiny Chapel of St Mary Magdalen in Ripon is the last remaining section of what was once the medieval hospital for the City. Founded in 1115 AD by Archbishop Thurstan of York, the hospital cared of any blind priests who had been born within the liberty of the City, but was also known as the Leper Hospital, this name harking back to the days when the disease was introduced by those returning from Crusade in the Holy Land. Legislation provided for born or living in Ripon to receive a garment and two pairs of shoes each year. Each day they were also to receive a loaf of bread and a ration of ale and meat (or fish on Fridays and during Lent), while Lepers from outside the city precincts were also cared for, given a meal and lodgings for the night. Sadly many of the chapel's original features fell casualty to the destructive attentions of Cromwell's Puritans during the Civil War; the stained glass is gone and the ornate Norman font, now residing near the doorway was found in a nearby field serving

Chapel of the Hospital of St Mary Magdalen, Ripon

as a cattle trough, while damage to the giant stone altar which bears a crack down the middle also dates to this time. However, in spite of centuries of neglect and the chapel variously used as a pig stye, cow byre and a storage barn, extensive restored carried out between 1985 and 1990 has ensured that this twelfth century gem is still in use as a chapel today.

Leper Squint, St Andrew's Church, Grinton, Swaledale

Often described as 'the Cathedral of the Dales' St Andrew's Church in Grinton has stood close to this important crossing point over the River Swale for more than 900 years, possibly longer as the oldest part of the Norman church may well have been superseded by an earlier Saxon church here.

Inside St Andrew's, set at an angle into the chancel wall is a 'leper squint', one of only two surviving examples in North Yorkshire (the other is in St Oswald's, Sowerby). The purpose of these oblique openings was to enable 'non-desirable' worshippers such as those suffering with leprosy, to view the altar and the elevation of the Host without coming into proximity with the rest of the congregation. The St Andrew's squint is a harsh reminder of the segregation of lepers, the scourge of medieval society, and denied participation in church services as well as contact with society at large. The 'unclean' were forced to wear distinctive clothing and carry a wooden clapper to warn of their approach, yet while some believed that leprosy was a punishment for sin, others however saw the suffering of lepers as similar to the suffering of Christ, and because lepers were enduring purgatory on earth, believed they would go directly to heaven when they died – spiritual consolation for those suffering in earthly misery.

Leyburn Shawl

The unusually named Leyburn Shawl stretches for a mile and three quarters along a pleasant grassy escarpment path, offering some of the most impressive views across to the Coverdale Fells and over rolling Wensleydale beyond. Associated with the failed escape attempt of Mary Queen of Scots who was once held prisoner in the vicinity, it was here that the Scots Queen finally lost all hope of liberty.

With a reasonable claim to the English throne, tracing her lineage through her Tudor grandmother Margaret, Henry VIII's older sister, Queen Elizabeth I deemed it prudent to hold Mary in custody lest her Catholic cousin make a bid for the crown. Arriving at Bolton Castle in mid-July 1568, though technically a prisoner, Mary did not have to endure the castle's terrible dungeon but instead was held her own suite of rooms and attended by numerous servants. During her six month imprisonment at Bolton Castle, it is said that she inscribed her name *Marie R* on one of the windows panes, scratched with a diamond ring, though sadly the glass was accidentally broken long ago.

As respite during her period of 'comfortable confinement' at Bolton Castle Mary was also allowed to go out hunting, under her gailor Lord Scrope's supervision of course, but nevertheless she was able to familiarise herself with the local area. This proved invaluable in aiding her later escape attempt when, evading her guards she climbed out of one of the castle windows and fled into the surrounding countryside, making for the nearest town of Leyburn. Mary's absence was soon noticed and a mounted search with dogs hastily mustered. As Mary could hear the hooves of her pursuers and the baying of the hounds ever closer, in her desperate flight her shawl caught on some briars and was dragged from her shoulders; with no time to go back and retrieve it, the betraying shawl led to her eventual recapture, and the name of the location where this drama supposedly played a reminder of Mary's ill-fated bid for freedom.

Leyburn Shawl, the supposed ill-fated escape route of Mary, Queen of Scots

Leyburn's Sham Castle

The fashion for classical ruins in English landscape architecture became a popular one in the eighteenth century. The wealthy elite undertaking 'The Grand Tour' returned romantically impressed with the ruined classical buildings they had encountered on their travel through Greece and Italy, and sought to mimic these themes with the creation of mock gothic ruins and ancient temples, scattered with seeming random abandon about the landscape of their grand estates.

An example of this craze for fanciful yet impractical ornamental features can be found in the

Set in the wooded grounds of Thornborough Hall, Leyburn's Sham Castle

grounds of Thornborough Hall in Leyburn where the small but perfectly formed 'sham' castle was built in 1863 at the behest of the hall's owner, Joseph Aloysius Hansom, the inventor of the hansom cab. The Sham Casle can still be seen, in a wooded area reached by a flight of stone steps behind the hall.

Little Emily's Bridge, Linton Village, Wharfedale

Amidst the group of cottages close to the lovely Linton Falls, on the original church footpath from Threshfield is the fourteenth century stone packhorse bridge spanning a stream known as Captain Beck. With low parapets and a stone-flagged surface, Little Emily's Bridge is unusual in that it features a 'squeeze stile', often used in the Yorkshire Dales to prevent livestock from passing through.

Linton is blessed with many river crossings, and almost as numerous are the legends attached to the naming of Little Emily's Bridge. One tale tells of how the bridge was named for a daughter of the Norton family who hid nearby at the time of the English Civil War, although the bridge may also have been named after a local girl called Emily Norton mentioned in Wordsworth's poem *The White Doe of Rylstone*, whose family were participants in the doomed 'Rising Of The North' in the reign of Queen Elizabeth I. There is however another suggestion that the name is purely the invention of novelist Halliwell Sutcliffe, writing in the early 1900s his historical romances set in the Yorkshire Dales drew on his knowledge of the legends and history of the area and introduced many fictional characters and places, later passing into local parlance as grounded in authentic antiquity.

The Loki Stone, St Stephen's Parish Church, Kirkby Stephen

Loki Stone, St Stephen's Church, Kirkby Stephen

The Norse equivalent of Satan, the god Loki is pictorially represented in carved relief in St Stephen's parish church in the small market town of Kirkby Stephen, nudging the

Cumbrian border. Of the three successive churches built on the footprint occupied by the existing church, it must have been into the stonework of the earliest Saxon predecessor that this relief of the Norse god was first incorporated, a horned figure depicted as bound and chained. Widely accepted as dating from the eighth century the Loki Stone harks back to the early Viking settlers in the vicinity and the Norse influence hereabouts before the arrival of Christianity. The stone itself has been much moved over the centuries and for many years was subject to the harsh weathering effect of the North Yorkshire elements while propped up outside the east end of the church. However, as one of only two known examples of its kind in Europe, (the second rare depiction is displayed in the Sculptured Stone Museum at Meigle, Perthshire) the stone's new position inside St Stephen's directly opposite the main south door is far more conducive to preserving the detail of this remarkable carving, showing Loki as a bound and vanquished demon, possibly adopted by the early church as positive representation of the triumph of good over evil and a reminder that Satan, in one guise or another, has always be prevalent in our ancestral psyche.

M

Maiden Castle, Grinton, Swaledale

Deep in Swaledale lead mining territory, on the southern slope of the dale west of Grinton is a unique piece of Iron Age architecture. Maiden Castle can lay claim to being the only known fort from this period with what seems to be a processional entrance, described by Jacquetta Hawkes in her 1978 *A Guide To The Prehistoric And Roman Monuments In England And Wales*:

"... *a curious place with a roughly circular bank and ditch approached from the east by a stone avenue. There are round barrows in the vicinity, and although the ditch lies outside the bank, it seems very probable that Maiden Castle is not a fort but some kind of sacred enclosure or meeting place.*"

It is probable that Maiden Castle came into being around 600 BC, with new settlers moving into the area to exploit the metal and mineral resources, as they would do for centuries to come. And while Maiden Castle may appear today as a dormant feature in the Dales landscape, it does have one further mysterious claim on our curiosity, as it is said that buried treasure lies within its enclosure – the legend of these hidden riches is explored under the letter 'X'.

Maiden's Bower Maze Mound, Asenby, near Thirsk

On the site of a supposed motte and bailey castle to the east of the Domesday village of Asenby, once part of the manor of Topcliffe, is the Maiden's Bower, the remains of one of England's forgotten turf mazes.

The tradition of turf mazes, convoluted paths cut into an area of short grass, was alluded to by Shakespeare in *A Midsummer Night's Dream*, though the patterns of many turf mazes are clearly very ancient. Speculation as to the purpose of such mazes has thrown up theories involving penitents sinners following the paths on their hands and knees, to village green mazes used for entertainment, particularly on 'high days and holidays' such as May Day.

While at Maiden's Bower there is no tangible labyrinth visible at ground level, viewed from the air traces of the Asenby maze are still apparent on the stepped mound, and it is said that on a summer's evening, if you happen upon the centre of the maze and kneel down you can hear the fairies singing.

Adjacent to the mound of Maiden's Bower are earthworks which formed the old castle, later superseded by a manor house called Cock Lodge, slightly to the north-west of the older site. And it was here that Henry fourth Earl of Northumberland was murdered. Having made himself unpopular in Yorkshire by his betrayal of Richard III, he later met with resistance from the local populace in levying a tax in 1489; on 28th April that year an angry mob collected and marched on Cock Lodge, and though the Earl sent for help he was the first man to be slain, many of his servant's suffering their master's fate.

A now forgotten turf maze once topped the mound of Maiden's Bower, visible above the earthworks which are the only remains of Cock Lodge

Malham Money Tree, Gordale Scar, Malhamdale

Reminiscent of tossing money into pools and wells for good luck, the tradition of making offerings to deities at wishing trees dates back hundreds if not thousands of years when it was believed that divine spirits inhabited the trunks and branches. It was also believed that pounding a coin into a special tree could be efficacious in relieving a person's illness, and conversely removing the coin would bring back the ailment.

On the footpath to Janet's Foss – see the Fairy Queen's entry under the letter 'J' – amidst the magical woodland hereabouts, a tree stump has been thus decorated with hundred's of lucky pennies, clearly a practice of some antiquity as some of the coins are very old.

Whoever said that money doesn't grow on trees?!

Marmion Tower, West Tanfield

On the banks of the River Ure, in the picturesque village of West Tanfield which lies just to the north of the ancient Cathedral City of Ripon, Marmion Tower is the fine fifteenth century gatehouse to what was once the fortified riverside manor house of Tanfield Castle, now long since vanished.

The tower was named for the lords of the manor, the Marmion family, many of their tombs and monuments gracing the adjacent thirteenth century church of St Nicholas. Constructed between 1350 and 1400 after a license to crenellate (permission to fortify a property) was granted in 1348 to Matilda, widow of John Marmion, the tower was remodelled several times and the current structure dates back to the mid-fifteenth century. Still discernable are the guardroom on the ground floor, and spiral staircase at the north-west corner leading up to the first floor where the upper rooms served as domestic chambers, with a decorative oriel window and even a garderobe (lavatory) that would have emptied into the adjacent River Ure.

Certainly the juxtaposition of medieval church and gatehouse set amongst the red-roofed cottages running down to the riverside is one of the loveliest views

Viewed from West Tanfield Bridge, the Marmion Tower stands to the left of the church tower, set amongst the red-roofed cottages of this lovely riverside village

hereabouts, best enjoyed from the vantage point of the old stone Tanfield Bridge, built in 1725 replacing the original ferry boat crossing the Ure here.

Mary Moreland's Grave, Bellerby, near Leyburn

The tale of Mary Moreland is a sad one. She lived in the village of Bellerby, just a mile and a half from the market town of Leyburn, at the end of the seventeenth century. Soon after her marriage, her husband suddenly and unexpectedly died, and Mary, in her grief took her own life by hanging herself. In accordance with custom and the law, as the bodies of suicides were denied burial in consecrated ground, Mary was to be interred on the boundary line of the village in an unmarked grave. However, while her body was being carried out of the parish, the ladder being used as a makeshift bier broke in two some 130 feet shy of the boundary in a field called Marleymire on the Richmond Road, and it was decided to bury Mary on the spot. Ever since this unfortunate incident the people of Bellerby and those of the neighbouring villages have disputed the boundary line between their settlements; as to the place where poor Mary was buried, this is still shown on the Ordnance Survey Map as 'Mary Moreland's Well'.

Mastiles Lane, monastic trackway between Kilnsey and Malham Moor

Mastiles Lane is part of the historic long distance monastic route once connecting the estates held by Fountains Abbey in the northern Lake District with the Mother House beyond Pateley Bridge. Once known as 'Strete Gate', on the Mastiles Lane section the remains of two medieval crosses still mark the route that once connected the Fountains monastic grange at Kilnsey with the sheep pastures on Malham Moor – wool an essential component of the monastic economy in the middle ages.

However, this route has been in use for at least two thousand years, if not longer, with the remains of a Roman marching camp straddling the course of the present-day route, a reminder of the first century AD Roman campaign to subjugate the rebellious Brigantes tribe who ruled much of this area.

Centuries later, after the dissolution of the monasteries, in the eighteenth century Mastiles Lane was still in use as a drove way, the route used to bring cattle from all over the north of England and from Scotalnd to local markets, and many other traders and travellers using the old lane as a through road to the cities and towns of Yorkshire and Lancashire.

Today local farmers still use Mastiles Lane for the movement of sheep and cattle between their fields, while many others simply enjoy the lane as part of a circular walk encompassing Kilnsey Crag and Malham Tarn, surrounded by the splendid views of the wide open moorland.

Megger Stones, Dent, Dentdale

Visible on the northern flank of Great Coum, rising to the south-west of Dent Town with its narrow cobbled streets and white-walled cottages, are a prominent collection of cairns known as the The Megger Stones. Built from large clusters of piled loose rock that may well have come from a nearby quarry, no-one quite knows their history, however it is possible they were constructed by nearby quarry workers in order to mark the route back down to Dent when visibility was reduced by misty conditions. Whatever their provenance, the views across Dentdale from this spot are quite breathtaking.

Mermaid Stone, Semmerwater, Raydale

The Mermaid and Carlow Stones, on the shore of Semmerwater

On the eastern shore of Semmerwater, Yorkshire's largest naturally formed lake and rich in it's own mythology, is the Mermaid Stone and it's close neighbour the Carlow Stone. Both Shap granite boulders were brought down by the glacier of the last Ice Age, however there is a tradition that the stones have lain in their present position ever since the Devil and a giant pelted one another with rocks thrown across the lake. To corroborate the legend, a huge boulder halfway up the slope of nearby Addleborough Hill is known as the Devil's Stone, and supposedly marked with the Devil's finger prints, though these are more probably prehistoric Cup-and-Ring marks. There is another demonic theory attached to the Mermaid and Carlow Stones however; rumoured to be the stones of a druidical altar and thrown from the top of Addleborough Hill to their current position in another show of strength by the Devil.

Semmerwater itself is strongly associated with local legend – that of a vanished town. It is said that a beggar once came to the town asking for shelter, but after being turned away at every door he eventually came to a farm on the nearby hillside where a kindly old couple gave him food and lodgings for the night. Next morning the beggar had vanished, but the whole town, excepting the poor old couple's cottage, had been punished for its lack of charity by being completely submerged underwater. Some believe that the beggar was actually an angel sent to test the goodness of the townsfolk, renowned for their selfishness and greed, and on finding them wholly wanting chanted:

> *Semerwater rise, Semerwater sink,*
> *And drown all the town but on little house*
> *Where they gave me meat and drink.*

In 1937, when the water levels of the lake were very low, an excavation uncovered an Iron Age settlement on what is now the bed of the lake, perhaps the submerged settlement remembered in legend.

Middleham Jewel

A tale to make all treasure hunters green with envy in 1985 Ted Seaton, who had been metal detecting near Middleham Castle, was on the point of calling it a day when he heard a faint signal. Digging down about 15 inches he unearthed what appeared to be an old make-up compact, however on closer inspection Mr Seaton realised he had found an exquisite piece of English Gothic jewellery, a diamond shaped gold pendant weighing three ounces set with a ten carot blue sapphire. Embossed with a picture of the Holy Trinity on the front and the Nativity on the reverse, it is thought that given the high value and prestige of the item the pendant may have been owned by the mother of Richard III, Cecily Neville, the piece dating to the fifteenth century and discovered in the environs of Middleham Castle, Richard III's childhood home.

Adjudged not to be Treasure Trove, the Middleham Jewel was saved for the nation following a campaign led by The Yorkshire Museum, launching a 2.5 million pound appeal to purchase the jewel, the highest amount paid at the time for any item of medieval jewellery. While the original is proudly on show in the Yorkshire Museum, a faithful facsimile of this beautiful object is appropriately displayed in St Alkelda's Church in Middleham.

Mohammed's Coffin, Weathercote Cave, Chapel-le-Dale

Weathercote Cave in Chapel-le-Dale, an area renowned for some of the deepest and longest cave systems in the British Isles, has been a popular venue for tourists since the eighteenth century. Indeed, one of the best descriptions of the cave dates to this era, found in *A Tour to the Caves in the Environs of Ingleborough and Settle* by the Reverend John Hutton (1780) in which he describes the cave as a "*stupendous subterranean cataract*". In 1781 enterprising tour guides were charging intrepid sightseers one shilling to visit the 108 foot deep cave and admire Mohammed's Coffin, the huge boulder suspended 77 feet above the cave floor. It was the Reverend Hutton who first gave this name to the wedged boulder, still a draw for tourists today, come to see the Chapel Beck thunder from the flooded cave above Mohammed's Coffin before plunging with a deafening roar, vanishing into the fissures below.

Monkey House, Swinton Estate, near Masham

This curious stone gazebo on the Swinton Estate near the charming market town of Masham once housed a seat overlooking the view up the valley of the River Burn. It was built "*with grateful mind by William Danby Esq AD 1832*", instigator of that other fabulous folly on the Swinton Estate mentioned under the letter 'I' – Ilton's Stonehenge.

In the absence of any tree loving primates hereabouts, the name of this folly has been attributed to the less than respectful term employed by the proletariat to describe the undeserving gentry in the nineteenth entury.

The 'Monkey House' on the Swinton Estate near Masham

My Love Lane, Thornthwaite with Padside, near Pateley Bridge

Amongst the tufts of grass on the verge at the Lane's junction with Greenhow Hill Road as it passes over Hanging Moor is the age old stone marker for 'My Love Lane'. Weathered and worn, the stone is at the head of the lane leading to the hamlet of Thornthwaite with Padside, and associated with the cursed lovers whose eternal, tearful wraiths wander these parts.

The story goes that one of the Ingleby family of Ripley Castle kept a number of mistresses dotted around the environs of the ancestral home. His favourite paramour was installed at the hamlet of Padside, between Blubberhouses and Pateley Bridge and a mere ten mile jaunt from the family seat. Padside Hall, the stone built house dating to the late sixteenth century was an Ingleby property, and as such perhaps presented a convenient venue for covert trysts, but the long-suffering Lady Ingleby eventually tracked down and confronted the Padside mistress, and finding her in the company of her unfaithful

Old stone marker for 'My Love Lane'

husband and presumably in a compromising situation, she cursed them both to a damned and restless afterlife. Within a year the realisation of Lady Ingleby's denouncement came to pass; while out hunting her husband was decapitated by the low hanging branch of a tree, while the mistress was carried off by a chill that had worsened to pneumonia. For many years after the double curse held; ghostly visions of a lady and gentleman walking in the Padside area were a frequent sight in the Victorian era, the disconcerted whispering wraiths forlornly disappearing into the mist.

N

Navvies Monument, All Saints Churchyard, Otley

The Navvies Monument, All Saint's churchyard, Otley

This evocative memorial in the churchyard of All Saint Parish Church, Otley, is a stone replica of the northern portal of the Bramhope Tunnel, and set up in 1913 to commemorate the 23 miners and excavators (navvies) killed during the tunnel's construction.

Proposals for a rail route from Leeds to the north and on to Scotland were first made in 1843, and after Royal Assent was given on 21st July 1845, construction commenced that year. However, contractor James Bray was faced with considerable technical problems in crossing the hills and valleys along the route, and the greatest challenge was to cut the Bramhope Tunnel. At a height of 25 feet, cut through just over two miles of solid rock, the men were working at depths of up to 290 feet; the 2,300 men and 400 horses involved in this work were all subject to the ever present risk of sudden rock falls, subsidence, flooding and collapse which could result in accidental death. One such victim commemorated on the Navvies Monument was James Myers who was buried in the Methodist Cemetery at Yeadon, a married man just 22 years old who '*died by an accident in the Bramhope Tunnel on the 14th day of April, 1848*' the following is inscribed on his gravestone:

> '*What dangers do surround*
> *Poor miners everywhere,*
> *And they that labour underground,*
> *They should be men of prayer.*'

The Navvies Monument is a poignant reminder of the human costs incurred with the advent of the glorious age of steam.

Necromancy on Gaterley Moor

On Gaterley Moor near the village of Greta Bridge, crossing the river of the same name just south of its confluence with the River Tees, a disturbing discovery was made in the year 1789 when two leaden tablets were found concealed beneath a heap of stones on top of a tumulus on the Moor. On one side of both tablets, divided into 81 small squares, were inscribed numerals ranging from from 1 to 81, and arithmetically proportioned so that the sum of each row – horizontally and diagonally, as well as perpendicularly – was equal to 369. Under one of these grids was drawn a depiction of a man named James Phillips, while on the reverse of both tablets several astrological or magical characters had been incised with the following inscription: *"I do make this, that James Phillip, John Phillip his son, Christopher Phillip and Thomas Phillip, his sons, shall fle Richemondshire, and nothing prosper with any of them in Richemondshire."* – *"I did make this, that the father James Phillip, John Phillip, and all kin of Phillip, and all the issue of them, shall come presently to utter beggery, and nothinge joy or prosper with them in Richemondshire."*

An account of the magical tables was sent to John E Brooke of the Somerset Herald's Office who was able to confirm that James Phillip was the second son of Henry Phillip of Brignall in the parish of Greta, and resident there in 1575. Though James had an elder brother Charles, who had two sons of his own, and James himself had five sons, the curse, presumably directed by someone who had suffered at the hands of James Phillip, was effective as no branch of the family flourished. After James's time the family ceased to prosper and within two generations the direct male line had failed and the estate passed into other hands through the marriage of a daughter; perhaps the magic had worked after all, as by the time of the Herald's Office enquiry the family line had been extinct for many years...

Nelson Connection, Holy Trinity Church, Wensley

In the church of The Holy Trinity in the village of Wensley, a stone's throw from the river Ure wending it way through Wensleydale, is the monument to a naval surgeon who was at the side of the dying national hero Horatio Nelson at the Battle of Trafalgar on 21st October 1805. High up on the wall of the south aisle the white marble monument commemorates Peter Goldsmith MD who lived in what is now The Secret Garden House on Grove Square in the nearby town of Leyburn. Coincidentally, Dr Goldsmith is buried in the churchyard at Wensley next to another naval surgeon, Thomas Maude. Though celebrated as a poet and essayist, in 1755 Maude was appointed surgeon on board the Barfleur, commanded by Lord Harry Powlett. Maude's favourable evidence given at a court-martial before which Lord Harry was tried at Portsmouth in October 1755 was so highly valued by his commander that upon Powlett's succession as sixth and last Duke of Bolton in 1765, he appointed Maude steward of his Yorkshire estates, the heart of which is Bolton Hall in Wensley.

Monument in Wensley's Holy Trinity to Peter Goldsmith MD - one of the surgeons attendant on the mortally wounded Lord Nelson at the Battle of Trafalgar

Nichol Stone, Conyers Lane, Akebar

Standing at the roadside between the villages Constable Burton and Patrick Brompton is the 'Nichol Stone'. Commemorating the foul deed of a highway robber who was hung at York for theft and murder committed on this stretch of the A684 known as Conyers Lane, the stone is inscribed with the now badly weathered words "*May 19, 1826 Do No Murder*".

Reputedly relating to the death of Nicholas Carter of Crakehall who was robbed and murdered on the spot by Leonard Wilkinson, Carter had been spotted by Wilkinson driving some livestock to Leyburn market back on that fateful May morning in 1826. Lying in wait and waylaying Carter on his return journey for the pocket full of money his cattle had made at sale, Wilkinson was subsequently brought to justice and hanged at the New Drop in St George's Fields, just outside York Castle walls on Monday 17th July 1826. His body was brought back and

The Nichol Stone or 'Murder Stone'

buried in unconsecrated ground outside the churchyard of Finghall Church, a stone's throw from where his crime was committed and where he is said to have sought sanctuary for a while.

Known locally as the 'Murder Stone', during the carriageway widening works carried out on this stretch of road some twenty years ago, it was found necessary to relocate the stone to a position further back on the verge. However, superstition runs strong in these parts and it was some time before the foreman could find enough men willing to even touch the Murder Stone, let alone move it. To this day those passing Nichol's Stone on particularly dark, moonless nights, and aware of the evil deed it commemorates report feeling an eerie foreboding, perhaps as a consequence of the murder committed here, or Wilkinson's restless wraith rising from his unconsecrated grave.

Norber Erratics, above Austwick village, near Settle

'Erratic' is the geological term applied to pieces of rock that differ in size and type from the rock native to the area in which they rest. With the coming of the warming period at the end of the Ice Age some 13,000 years ago, the glaciers and ice sheets eventually melted, depositing rocks sometimes hundreds of miles from their original position. Varying in size from pebbles to large boulders, the Norber Erratics certainly fall into the latter category.

At Norber the erratic boulders were carried by ice flowing out of Crummackdale and over the brow of the hill, and though they probably only travelled about a mile, the journey would have taken thousands of years. Acting as sort of natural umbrella, these erratics composed of Silurian sandstone sheltered the soluble limestone on which they rested from the eroding effects of rainwater, and while the surface of the surrounding exposed bedrock was lowered by the weathering of the elements, the erratics were left standing on small plinths of protected limestone.

These much visited and precariously perched boulders are certainly one of Mother Nature's true curiosities.

Novelist's inspiration for Mad Mrs Rochester – Norton Conyers House, Wath, near Ripon

The distinctive Dutch-style gables of Norton Conyers, along with the other Stuart and Georgian architectural additions, belie the late medieval origins of this manor house, which over the years has been honoured with such noteworthy visitors as King Charles I, in 1633, and the future King James II and his second wife Mary of Modena, in 1679 (the room and the bed they traditionally used are still on display). And of course most pertinent to this entry, Charlotte Brontë stayed at Norton Conyer in 1839.

The moment when the insane Mrs Rochester finds Jane Eyre's wedding veil – "It removed my veil from its gaunt head, rent it in two parts, and, flinging both on the floor, trampled on them..." Chapter XXV Charlotte Brontë's 'Jane Eyre'

During her stay Charlotte was fascinated by her host's stories of a mad woman who had been confined in the attic of the hall sometime in the 18th century. Eight years later, when Charlotte came to write *Jane Eyre* she remembered this story, and the madwoman of Norton Conyers became the model for the psychotic Mrs Rochester. Many details of Norton Conyers were also incorporated in her descriptions of Mr Rochester's house, Thornfield Hall, including the nearby rookery, the sunken fence in front of the house, and in 2004 the discovery of a blocked staircase linking the first floor to the attics mirrored the staircase vividly described by Brontë in the novel, the real life hidden flight of stairs that were the inspiration for those leading from Mr Rochester's grand bedroom to his mad wife's attic prison. Thankfully Norton Conyers has never been subject to the fiery fictitious destruction that befell Thornfield Hall, and can be visited on special open days throughout the summer months.

O

Old Age

Dales folk are a tough breed, reflected in some of the staggering ages recorded on gravestones and in parish registers county wide.

By far the oldest contender is Henry Jenkins of Bolton on Swale who is said to have been 169 years old at his death! His grave, marked by a black marble obelisk in the churchyard of St Mary's is inscribed thus:

"Blush not, marble, to rescue from oblivion the memory of Henry Jenkins, a person obscure in birth, but of a life truly memorable, for he was enriched with the goods of nature if not of fortune, and happy in the duration if not the variety of his enjoyments. And though the partial world despised and disregarded his low and humble state, the equal eye of Providence beheld and blessed it with a patriarch's health and length of days, to teach mistaken man these blessings are entailed on temperance, a life of labour, and a mind at ease. He lived to the amazing age of 169; was interred here, December 6, 1670, and had this justice done to his memory, 1743."

Monument to 169 year old Henry Jenkins in St Mary's churchyard, Bolton on Swale

Jenkins claimed to have been born in 1501, although his birth date cannot be verified as the compulsory requirement for parish registers to be kept was not introduced until 1538. However Chancery Court records show that in 1667 he stated on oath that he was aged *"one hundreth fifty and seven or thereabouts"* (perhaps advanced age accounted for the discrepancy in his estimation), though when asked by the judge which notable battles he could remember, he named Flodden Field fought in 1513, and further claimed to have carried arrows for the English archers. His burial record in St Mary's register dated 9th December 1670 describes Jenkins as "*a very aged and poor man*". Perhaps not spiritually poor though, as in 1829 the journal The Mirror of Literature claimed that if Jenkins had been truthful about his age, and followed his legal obligations, during his life he would have changed his religion eight times, between the reigns of Henry VII and Charles II.

Another example of Dales longevity rests in the churchyard of the now ruined St Mary the Virgin, Pateley Bridge where the grave of Mary Myers records that she died in 1743 reputedly at the age of 120 years, her life spanning the reigns of the six Stuart monarchs until the second Hanoverian George II occupied the throne.

Though not quite as old as Mary Myers, the memorial cut into the base of the porch of St Nicholas Church in West Tanfield tells us that Ralph Bourne would have been 113 years old when he died. Born in 1615, having weathered the English Civil War, experienced Cromwell's Puritan reign and survived the Great Plague, he lived on into the first year of George II's reign.

Memorial to Ralph Bourne who lived and died in West Tanfield, aged 113 years!

However, a concentration of centenarians seemed to hail from the villages around Kirkby Malzeard, where the churchyard of St Andrew's holds the remains of George Wharton of Laverton who died in 1844 at the ripe old age of 112, while the parish register gives further details of Jonathan Wood of Kirkby Malzeard who died in 1738 aged 100, and in 1789 the burial of 108 year old William Prest of Galphay; not to be outdone, in 1816 Thomason Myers, also of Galphay was buried after attaining his 100th birthday – perhaps a relation of the long-lived Mary Myers of Pateley Bridge?

Old Boots, Unicorn Hotel, Ripon

Facing onto Ripon's bustling market square the Unicorn Hotel has been in the business of selling beer since 1379. However, 'Old Boot's tenure at the inn dates to the 1760s. To give him his real name, Tom Crudd, also known as Thomas Spence, was a servant at the Unicorn Inn and was responsible for assisting weary travellers with the removal of their boots, usually greeting them with a pair of slippers in one and hand and a boot jack in the other, hence his nickname. However, Tom was clever enough to supplement his wage by making play of his extraordinary appearance, namely his enormous nose and chin. Thanks to these facial abnormalities (one imagines comparable to Mr Punch) Tom was able to acquire extra tips by demonstrating how he could hold a coin in between his nose and chin, and cannily keeping hold of the money as payment for his performance. Still resident in the Unicorn, the benign ghost of 'Old Boots' is said to still haunt the hotel but it's not known if he still performs his pecuniary party piece!

Old Mother Shipton's Cave, Knaresborough

At Knaresborough the dual curiosities of witch and wishing well are perfectly combined in 'Old Mother Shipton's Cave' and the associated 'Petrifying' or 'Dropping' well.

The Unicorn Hotel, Ripon - the haunt of 'Old Boots'

Known as a great prophetess and soothsayer in the reign of Henry VIII, born Ursula Southeil (she later married a man called Toby Shipton), according to legend Ursula was actually born in her now famous cave. As well as predicting the Great Fire of London, the building of the Crystal Palace and the Crimean War, Old Mother Shipton's prophecies alluded to many modern events and phenomena, the advent of the motor car and aircraft, ironclad warships and submarines, and it would seem even the Internet was foreseen in her verses:

> "Carriages without horses shall go,
> And accidents fill the world with woe.
> Around the world thoughts shall fly
> In the twinkling of an eye.
> Under water men shall walk,
> Shall ride, shall sleep, shall talk.
> In the air men shall be seen,
> In white, in black, in green;
> Iron in the water shall float,
> As easily as a wooden boat.

Gold shall be found and shown
In a land that's now not known."

Today a statue of Old Mother Shipton sits in her cave, while nearby the Dropping Well is adorned with all kinds of porous items which have been rendered into rock; from teddy bears, dolls and items of clothing, the local spring dripping over the small cliff above picking up the minerals from the earth and transforming the objects into stone. In 1923 when Queen Mary visited the cave she was so impressed by the spectacle of the Well that she left her shoe to be petrified – it now takes pride of place in the Cave museum. Other noteworthies to leave personal items for petrification include Agatha Christie who left her handbag, as well as John Wayne who left his Stetson cowboy hat. Incidentally the Petrifying Well is said to be England's oldest visitor attraction, first opening its gates in 1630, and enduringly popular today.

Old Peculier

No, the peculiar spelling isn't a typo, as in this instance the 'Peculier Court of Masham' was an ecclesiastical court established by the Archbishop of York in the twelfth century enabling the parish to govern its own affairs, independent of the rest of the diocese. Derived from the Norman French word for 'particular' rather than 'odd', the chairman of this Peculier court is known as 'The Official' and a special seal marks his decisions of approval.

This seal may well be familiar to some beer drinkers, as the image appears on the label of Theakston's Old Peculier beer, brewed in Masham (pronounced Massam) since the 1890s, and while no record of the original seal exists, the seal used today was granted by George III and is thought to be based on the original. It has been suggested that the kneeling man in the centre of the seal may represent Roger de Mowbray, lord of the lands and estates of Mashamshire and held prisoner by Saladin while on crusade in the Holy Land. Having been redeemed by the Knights Templar, in gratitude Roger gave the living of the church at Masham to the church of St Peter in York. However, the Archbishop of York was not overjoyed with this gift as it meant that he would now be responsible for administering the law in that district, and not relishing the prospect of a difficult journey from York through thick, bandit infested forests he came up with the solution of freeing Masham of *'all the customs and claims of his archdeacons and officials'* thus the Peculier Court came into being.

Though fulfilling a somewhat symbolic function today, in the past the Court used to have a great deal of local power, and the following are some examples of the offence that came before it:

- not coming to church enough
- keeping a hat on at communion
- bidding the churchwardens to do their worst on being asked to go to church
- not bringing their children to be baptised
- husband and wife living apart
- swearing
- brawling and scolding
- harbouring Roman Catholic priests
- carrying a dead man's skull out of the churchyard and laying it under the head of a person to charm them to sleep
- drunkenness

For many years Theakston's Old Peculier was affectionately referred to as Yorkshire's 'Lunatic's Broth', perhaps then the last offence in the list is still the most apt today!

Our Lady of the Crag, Knaresborough

This Marian wayside shrine (dedicated to the Virgin Mary) lays on the route leading to the now ruined Trinitarian priory, decimated by the Scots in 1318 and finally dissolved, a victim of the Reformation in 1538. All that survives of the priory today is part of the south precinct wall in the garden of Abbey House. The shrine however is in much better shape.

Built by 'John the Mason' in 1408, in thanks for the miraculous escape of his son who emerged unscathed from a rock fall in his father's quarry, John the Mason may have had a less than altruistic motive in mind when building the chapel as clearly the work of this master craftsman displayed in the carved altar, vaulted ceiling, roof bosses and gargoyles must have been an excellent advertisement for his deftness with mallet and chisel.

Appearing as though created from the crag itself, the shrine is still open to visitors and pilgrims today, the impressive carving of a larger than life sized knight giving rise to the supposition that the shrine was in fact the cave inhabited by the hermit and saint Robert of Knaresborough. St Robert's cave is actually located a little over a mile downstream from Our Lady of the Crag – see the last entry under the letter 'I' for more of the saintly Robert's cave.

Owl or Pussycat...? Masham

Perched high on the south facing wall of an old stone house in Masham's College Lane is the pitch covered wooden carving of a black owl – though on closer inspection the creature does display some distinct feline qualities...

Masham's 'meowl'?

This somewhat bug-eyed hybrid appears to have the head of a cat and the body of an owl – a 'meowl' perhaps?! – and is attached to Barn Owl Cottage. Clearly unusual in its colouring as black barn owls are very, very rare, their plumage usually of a rich apricot colour, much folklore and tradition is attached to the Barn Owl, the custom of of nailing a dead owl to a barn door to ward off evil and protect against lightening strikes persisting into the nineteenth century. Barn owls were also said to have possessed the uncanny knack of predicting the weather, the creature's screech a sure indicator of storms or an approaching spell of cold weather, although the screech or call of an owl flying past the window of a sick person could also presage imminent death. It was also said that owls were the only creatures able to live with ghosts, so if an owl is found nesting in an abandoned house, the place must be haunted! However, in parts of northern England it is good luck to see an owl, so perhaps Masham's black owl is a feature intended to favour fortune, in spite of its long, eerie shadow cast at night by the adjacent street light...

P

Paulinus Plunging Early Christians, St Anne's Church, Catterick Village

As depicted in one of the stained glass windows of St Anne's Church at Catterick Village, Paulinus, seventh century Christian missionary and the first Bishop of York utilised the waters of the River Swale for the en masse baptism of the local pagan Anglo Saxons population. The Venerable Bede in his monumental *Ecclesiastical History of England* tells us that Saint Paulinus baptised large numbers of converts in the River Swale somewhere between Easby and Catterick Bridge, they following the example of the newly converted Edwin, the Saxon king of Northumbria

Saint Paulinus carried out at least two further mass baptisms in Swaledale, the first near Brompton and the second at Brafferton, where it is said ten thousand converts entered the river to be baptised, and where no casualty resulted, in spite of the press of the great number of new Christians. In fact, those who entered with some "*feeblenesse and infirmitie*" returned from the river "*whole and reformed*". Not surprisingly this led to the river becoming known as the Holy River of St Paulinus.

St Paulinus busy baptising in the River Swale, shown in the stained glass from the south aisle of St Anne's Church, Catterick Village

Pennine Light, Coverdale and Wensleydale

An ethereal, flickering light defying explanation has been disconcerting motorists in the vicinity of East Scrafton in Coverdale for many years now. Known as the 'Pennine Light' this intense beam seen floating down the middle of the road and often mistaken for an approaching motorcyclist has been associated with the nearby St Simon's Well, a spring of water formerly used as a healing bath. The ruins of an oratory chapel dedicated to the saint close to the well is traditionally held as the resting place of St Simon the Canaanean and Apostle, and whether these holy remains are the catalyst for generating the unearthly glow, perhaps this is the same dazzling globe seen in the environs of West Witton, possibly migrating across from the neighbouring dale. Here the descriptions of sightings of 'earth lights' are similar to the haunting floating lights familiar to ancient peoples and regarded as fairies by the Celts, though the Welsh knew them as 'corpse candles'. In West Witton the light appears as a dazzling, glowing ball emitting an extremely high pitched sound not unlike a dog whistle, but vanishing on the approach of people or vehicles – and it has to be said, often seen around closing time!

Pet Cemeteries

While evidence of ritualistic canine burials date back to the Paleolithic period when pet dogs were sometimes interred in the tombs of their owners, perhaps ensuring the deceased had a guardian or companion in the afterlife, it was Queen Victoria who was responsible for starting the 'fashion' for dog cemeteries in the grounds of stately homes in the nineteenth century. A great animal lover, many of the Queen's four legged companions

A group of tiny headstones in the pet cemetery in the grounds of Swinton Castle

were buried in the grounds of her beloved Osborne House on the Isle of Wight, and a number of her favourite animals were also interred in the pet cemetery at Windsor Castle, including many dogs immortalized with life-size bronze statues. However, examples from the Dales are somewhat more low-key yet nonetheless lovingly sentimental.

The Thorp Perrow estate, just to the north of the village of Snape boasts a fine arboretum, and here beneath the spreading canopy alongside one of the lovely woodland walks are a touching collection of miniature graves marking the burial spots of various beloved dogs. A further collection of tiny headstones can also be seen in the grounds of Swinton Park, close to the riverside market town of Masham, the ancestral home of the Danbys and later the Cunliffe-Lister family, these fond memorials are a touching sight.

Pinker's Pond, Middleham Low Moor

Besides the road winding its way up through Middleham, the childhood home of Richard III, out on to Low Moor leading into Coverdale is Pinkers Pond. Usually a dried out expanse of mud in summer, the reedy lake that appears in winter and enjoyed by ducks and the odd swan was in fact created in the early twentieth century when the adjacent road from Middleham to Carlton was upgraded from the original track. Presumably the dearth of any ripples in the summer months is the result of natural seepage through the limestone rock proliferating throughout the geology of the Dales, but nonetheless Pinker's Pond makes for a delightful spot for a picnic, with no risk of drowning!

Pinker's Pond, surprisingly full at the beginning of Summer

Plumpton Rocks, near Knaresborough

Plumpton Rocks are an extensive range of weathered and contorted gritstone outcrops, part of which form the natural backdrop to the large and picturesque gardens designed by Daniel Lascelles in 1760 for the Harewood Estate.

Turner made two oil studies of 'Plompton Rocks' following his first visit to Yorkshire in 1797, and the pair of paintings commissioned by the 1st Earl of Harewood still hang in the Saloon at Harewood House.

Today visitors can enjoy this historic landscaped garden captured by Turner, exploring the 30 acres of parkland with tranquil lake side walks and romantic woodland trails through bluebells and rhododendrons when in season.

Polly Peachum's Tower, Wensley, Wensleydale

Perched on Capple Bank, overlooking the river at Wensley stand the ruins of a two storey stone tower, built directly opposite Bolton Hall across the dale, the ancestral home of the Dukes of Bolton.

The tower was constructed at the behest of the Charles Paulet, the 3rd Duke of Bolton who had become infatuated with celebrated actress and singer of the London stage Lavinia Fenton. Renowned for her role as 'Polly Peachum' in John Gay's *The Beggar's Opera*, their affair began in 1728, Lavinia bearing the Duke three sons, and after the demise of Lady Bolton in 1751 the Duke finally made the actress his Duchess.

Polly Peachum's Tower was intended as a summer pavilion in which Lavinia could rehearse her singing undisturbed, however it is said that the true motive was to spare the ageing duke from having to listen to her incessant voice, in her tower 'Polly' could perform to her heart's content – well out of his lordship's earshot at Bolton Hall!

Another tangible reminder of the Duke and Lavinia's love affair can be found inside Holy Trinity Church in Wensley, where the Bolton Family pew is actually fashioned from a double opera box taken from Drury Lane Theatre in the eighteenth century. One of Hogarth's paintings depicts a scene at Drury Lane with the Duke sat in one of the opera boxes, and when the theatre was refurbished the Duke acquired the box and had it installed in Wensley church, a curiosity that remains to this day.

Powder House, Langthwaite, Arkengarthdale

Arkengarthdale cuts through the eastern half of a major lead mining field from which ore has been extracted for over a thousand years. Today most of the mining structures have now disappeared leaving only the grass covered spoil heaps, however the presence of the Powder House, isolated in the middle of a field a safe distance from the CB Inn, is an appreciable reminder of the industry once carried out in these parts under the auspices of the Bathurst family.

Now used as a farm building, the Powder House was originally used to store the explosive black powder so essential in lead mining, but in case of any accidental explosion was sited within a cordon of uninhabited land. Built in 1807, specifically designed with strong walls and a relatively weak roof so that any accidental blast would be directed upwards, the hexagonal shape of the building was believed to have special properties for containing explosions.

In 1656 the valley of Arkengarthdale was bought by Dr John Bathurst, who was Oliver Cromwell's doctor. The estate remained in the Bathurst family for four generations, and his descendants did much to develop the lead mining industry in the dale, especially Charles Bathurst who was lord of the manor in the eighteenth century and who gave his name not only to the lead from the mines, but also the curiously named CB Inn – the local and abbreviated name for the Charles Bathurst Inn.

Pudding Pie Hill, Sowerby, near Thirsk

With its parish boundary merging with that of neighbouring Thirsk, Sowerby could be described as a suburb of that town, however retaining its wide tree lined Front Street with some fine Georgian facades, Sowerby keeps its own identity.

When 'Sorebi' was mentioned in the Domesday Book in 1086, the round barrow a short distance from the tiny stone bridge crossing Cod Beck had already been a feature of the landscape for at least 3,000 years. Known as 'Pudding Pie Hill', so named for its resemblance to a pie or a pudding, the barrow was excavated in 1855 by Lady Frankland Russell. Found to contain the burial of a saxon warrior along with two other skeletons and associated coins and possessions, the Pudding Pie barrow is a burial site of a type called a 'bowl barrow' and dating to the Late Neolithic-Bronze Age period. The discovery of cremated bones, funeral urns and weapons at varying depths suggest the re-use of the barrow with the later burial dating to the sixth century, and as the upper most of the three skeletons was described as '*of a warrior apparently of more than ordinary size*', perhaps he was a lofty relative of the unusually tall skeleton discovered in a sixth century grave near the site of Thirsk Castle, whose bones indicate he would have stood 7 feet tall in life.

The imaginatively named Pudding Pie Hill, Sowerby

Even before excavations confirmed Pudding Pie Hill as a site of ancient burial, the mound had mythical associations. It was said that if you ran nine times around the hill then climbed to the top and stuck a knife in the ground you could hear fairy voices from within. However these tales don't seem to peterb the local children who enjoy the the opportunity the hill presents for excellent sledging in the winter.

Q

Quakers

As the birthplace of Quakerism, '1652 Country' holds a special place in the history of the Quaker movement, and draws many visitors each year. It was in the north of England that the message of the movement's founder George Fox (1624-1691) first took root, Fox travelling the length and breadth of the North and East Ridings of Yorkshire between 1651-52, and after preaching at Firbank Fellside (see the entry under the letter 'F' for 'Fox's Pulpit') the early converts, known as the 'First Publishers of Truth', spread out across the country.

At Brigflatts, near Sedbergh, the oldest Meeting House in the north of England was established after Fox first visited the hamlet in 1652. Land for the Meeting House was purchased at the cost of ten shillings and within the simplicity of the white-washed exterior, very much in the style of local farmhouses of that period, there was even a dog pen at the foot of the stairs to accommodate any sheep dogs accompanying their masters to meeting. Still a venue for Friends' Meetings, the peace and tranquillity of the Brigflatts Meeting House certainly leaves a lasting impression, receiving more than 2,000 visitors a year from all over the world.

Quarantine

In the summer of 1665 the Bubonic Plague broke out in London and rapidly spread to the rest of the country throughout the following year. The plague or 'Black Death' had recurrently afflicted England since the fourteenth century, and at its zenith in 1348 the disease was responsible for the deaths of more than one third of Britain's population. Though the infection was carried by the fleas which infested black rats, the terrified population had no idea as to the epidemic's true cause, many attributing the horrific visitation to the wrath of God, and understandably resorted to quarantine measures in an attempt to prevent contagion.

There are still a number of extant reminders to these quarantine efforts around the Dales – the first the 'Plague Cross' situated a mile and a quarter from Bedale on the Crakehall road. A round stone socket supporting a portion of a plain stone shaft, also known as the 'White Cross' this vergeside monument is said to have marked the spot where neighbouring villagers would meet to exchange goods during the time of the Black Death, and in an effort to prevent the spread of infection money was left in a bowl of vinegar, a primitive disinfectant. The White Cross has also been associated with the alternate location for a market set up by traders from Bedale when an outbreak of cattle disease ravaged the area in the medieval period, the stone therefore imbued with a double dose of infective connotations.

A second example of a 'plague cross', and still retaining the stone quarantine trough, can be found at the Alne crossroads on the road running north-west from York to Brafferton. A venue for barter that was safely removed from the populace when an outbreak of plague was raging in Yorkshire in 1604, villagers from the surrounding district would come to this stone cross and leave money in a vinegar solution in exchange for food. Today the rain water filled trough still contains coins as people now regard it as something of a wishing well.

In Giggleswick village, less than a mile from the charming market town of Settle, a 'Plague Stone' commemorates the outbreak in 1597 of the 'Settle Plague' and can be seen opposite the entrance to Close House, near the Craven Arms Hotel (formerly The Old Station Inn). Sunk into the ground before the inscribed tablet is a stone with a square socket, traditionally marking the boundary

The 'White Cross' on the road between Crakehall and Bedale

The quarantine trough attached to the The Plague Cross at Alne crossroads now holds the happier associations of a wishing well

of the infected area. Here again food and other necessities were deposited, while the quarantined left their payment in the vinegar filled hollow in an attempt to prevent the disease from spreading outside the town.

A further reminder of bleaker times past, during the Plague's 1636 visitation the north of England was particularly badly affected, and with the fairs and markets of Barnard Castle and the neighbouring towns 'cried down' something of a quarantine marketplace came into being around a grooved, roughly pyramid shaped boulder known as the 'Butterstone' on the moor above the village of Cotherstone, close to the Cotherstone to Bowes road. Here not only were butter and eggs placed in the vicinity of the aptly named stone for exchange, but also sacks of wheat left along with tethered livestock. Upon the Butterstone, known as a "cup rook" was placed a basin kept constantly full of water, into which the buyer would drop coin commensurate with his own estimation and honesty. As for the village of Cotherstone, the virtual depopulation of the settlement was attributed to the irreverence of the villagers who were said to christen calves in open contempt of the sacrament of baptism. There is in fact a stone cross base standing in the field to the south of the Cotherstone to Romaldkirk road, known locally as the 'Christening Stone' where tradition says that calfs were christened each May Day.

The Plague Stone, St Mary's churchyard, Richmond

Though this consecrated stone was used for the "resting" of coffins en-route to Romaldkirk for burial, clearly the supposed sacrilegious practices of the local farming community in mediaeval times echoed down the ages, as the later decimation of Cotherstone's population was seen as a divine retribution and punishment for their past Godless ways. However to this day coins are still left on the Butterstone, a reminder of the terrible days when the plague cast a dark shadow over this part of Teesdale.

In the market town of Richmond, in spite of the quarantine measures undoubtedly taken, the outbreak of plague in the late 1500s caused immense suffering to the populace here. With the death of over 1,000 townsfolk –

probably about half the population of Richmond at the time, the unmarked stone set beside St Mary's Church is said to commemorate the deaths of all those buried there.

Queen of Hearts, Ripon Cathedral

Clearly the young Charles Lutwidge Dodgson – better known under his pen name Lewis Carroll – was susceptible to the impressionistic ecclesiastic environments of his upbringing. His inspiration for the Cheshire Cat in *Alice's Adventures in Wonderland* has already been mentioned under the letter 'C', but further characters in the story may have been drawn from some of decorative features in Ripon Cathedral where Dodgson's father was a Canon from 1852-1868. His muse for the foul-tempered Queen of Hearts can be found amongst the lofty gilded corbels in the Cathedral's south transept, and a carving decorating one of the misericord seats found in the chancel choir stalls showing a griffin in hot pursuit of a rabbit down a hole possibly the inspiration for the eternally late White Rabbit.

Queen's Gap, beneath Leyburn Shawl, Leyburn

About two miles from Bolton Castle, beneath the ridge of Leyburn Shawl famed as the failed escape route taken by Mary Queen of Scots and mentioned under the letter 'L', there is a narrow way, or pass, which is commonly known as the 'Queen's Gap'. The story goes that here the fleeing Queen of Scots was recaptured after her attempted escape from Bolton Castle where she had been detained on the orders of Elizabeth I. Since that day this place has been known as the spot where Mary's brief taste of freedom was curtailed for good. Over the succeeding nineteen years Mary was held in 'comfortable confinement around the country', and while she tried to arrange a face-to-face meeting with her cousin Elizabeth, the Virgin Queen never set eyes on her Roman Catholic rival, and Mary's implication in Papist plots to murder Elizabeth sealed her fate, Mary executed at Fotheringhay Castle on 8th February 1587.

R

Rey Cross, westbound layby A66, between Bowes and North Stainmore

Now occupying a lay-by on the A66 some five miles west of Bowes, the Rey Cross was once the marker denoting the boundary between the Dark Age kingdoms on either side of the Pennines, with Viking Danes holding sway in the east and Norwegian Vikings to the west. However, the Rey Cross also marks the the spot where the colorfully named Eric Bloodaxe fell in battle.

The most famous Viking of his era and the last of the Viking kings of England, Bloodaxe was the fearsome red-headed ruler of the kingdom of Northumbria and is said to haunt the site of his last engagement, his final battle cry carried on the howling Pennine wind.

In 954 AD Eric met a sticky end along with his son Haeric and his brother Ragnald at the Battle of Stainmore; betrayed by Earl Oswulf who had treacherously led Eric to believe he could rely on his martial support, the ancient stone cross is a reminder of the demise of Bloodaxe ending the Viking domination of the Jorvik kingdom, the might of the Norsemen not to be felt again until the accession of King Cnut.

Originally standing at over 10 feet high, the Rey Cross is today sadly minus the wheel-head and upper section of its shaft, these long since having disappeared, leaving just the worn stump socketed into a more modern base. In 1989, taking advantage of the widening of the A66 through Stainmore, an excavation was carried out; though archaeologists found no bones at the site of the Rey Cross, it remains possible that Eric's burial place might still lay undiscovered elsewhere on remote Stainmore...

The Rey Cross

Rhyming Fountain, Lofthouse, near Pateley Bridge

After crossing the scenic moorland of Fountains Earth Moor where breathtaking panoramic views of Upper Nidderdale unfold, the road steeply drops into

The drinking fountain at Lofthouse offers rhyming health advice!

Lofthouse village. Here close to the Methodist Chapel dated 1778 stands the village Drinking Fountain, the original eighteenth century old stone octagonal trough incorporated into the remodelled drinking fountain which was re-dedicated in 1920 to the memory of local men who lost their lives in the First World War. The inscription on the fountain's south face reads: "*A pint of cold water three times a day is the surest way to keep the doctor away. Whoso thirsteth let him come hither and drink*", while on the eastern facing side, replete with water tap, is the the inscription '*If you want to be healthy, wealthy and stout, use plenty of water inside and out*"!

Ripon Jewel

Discovered close to Ripon Cathedral in 1976, the 'Ripon Jewel', just over an inch in diameter, dates to the seventh century and is therefore contemporary with the founding of Ripon Cathedral by St Wilfrid in 672. Backed with plain gold sheet and with four settings for gems fashioned from strips of gold on the front, at the points of the cross are squares of amber, with smaller triangular garnets set in between, however the central setting and inner arcs of inlay are now sadly missing.

While the 'Ripon Jewel' is of a type of inlaid jewellery fashionable during Saxon period and worn by only the highest in the land, the possession of a king, noble or an important churchmen, the cross design does however suggest some ecclesiastical function, perhaps to embellish a reliquary casket, a cross or some other church ornament, and perhaps ordered by St Wilfrid himself.

One has to wonder, if Wilfrid were alive today, whether he would have ordered a different kind of 'Ripon Jewel', as in September 1999 the Cathedral was the first in the country to launch – and bless – its own brand of beer called 'Ripon Jewel'. Granted a license to sell the 5.8 per cent proof ale in the cathedral shop, the bottled beer made by Daleside Breweries in Harrogate was officially blessed by the Dean of Ripon, the Very Reverend John Methuen in a special ceremony followed by a procession carrying the beer through the streets for a civic toast and tasting. And while the church is firm in its stance against alcohol abuse, it recognises that '*a drink in moderation is a gift from God*' – a prayer and a pint perhaps?!

Ripon Rowels

In the reign of Henry III (1216-1272) Ripon was especially famous for the manufacture of fine spurs: '*As true steel as Ripon rowels*' became a proverbial expression throughout England to denote honesty and courage.

It was said that Ripon rowels – rowels being the spiked revolving disc at the end of a spur – would strike through a shilling, and rather break than bend. A prestigious gift for a king, when James I passed through the town in 1617 enroute to Scotland, he was presented with a pair of spurs valued at five pounds.

Today the memory of Ripon's renowned industry lives on in various guises, with the Ripon Rowel Handicap run at Ripon's Racecourse, The Ripon Rowel Rotary Club and a plethora of other bodies and organisations adopting the name, and of course the Ripon Rowel Walk – a circular trail around the city encompassing South Stainley, Markington and Masham with Fountains Abbey and Studley Royal Water Gardens also forming part of the route, the waymark signs for which are of course the circular Rowel logo.

Rock Castle, Bellerby, near Leyburn

In a field bordering the road running from Leyburn to Bellerby stand the remains of Rock Castle, the gradual deterioration of the ruins hastened by a lightning strike some years ago. Built on rocks near the edge of a wood, this was probably a Pele or watch tower, one of a number of small fortified keeps or tower houses scattered throughout the border territory of northern England and dating to the violent era of incursions by marauding Scots. There are tales of a secret tunnel connecting Rock Castle to Bellerby's Old Hall on the village main street, and tradition has it that the captive Mary Queen of Scots was to have hidden at Old Hall on her flight toward to Richmond enroute to her native land, and that a band of Scots guards was stationed at the house, the seat of the aptly named Scott family, loyal to Mary's cause, waiting to receive her and assist in her escape from Bolton Castle. However, as the Scots Queen's bid to regain her freedom proved futile we can assume that neither Hall nor tunnel nor castle were ever graced with her royal presence...

Romano Recycling

Within just ten years of invading the South of England in 43 AD the Romans had moved into the North and set up client kingdoms, and while the primary purpose of their occupation was military: to quash local rebellions and Scottish invasions, nevertheless evidence of everyday Roman activity can be found dotted around the Dales, recycled and re-styled to fit in with the succeeding way of life after the Empire's eventual withdrawal from these shores in the late fourth century AD, Roman troops recalled to defend their own domestic borders.

Many Roman remnants seemed to find their way into the fabric of churches. A Roman carving of the god Mercury can be found built into the stonework of the north aisle of St Andrew's Church, Aldborough, once the important Roman garrison town of Isurium Brigantum; St Andrews is possibly built on the site of a Roman Temple of Mercury, the statue of the winged-heeled god having been found nearby.

Within the now ruined old church of St Mary at Brignall near Barnard Castle, the altar from a Roman temple was found, an unusual occurrence because it is rare that such an intrinsically pagan relic, once the focus of heathen worship, should be reused in a Christian church.

Carving of the Roman god Mercury, now incorporated into the interior stonework of St Andrew's Church, Aldborough

A similar utilisation can be found in St Giles Church, Bowes, situated next to the ruins of the medieval Bowes Castle, itself built on the site of a former Roman fort called *Lavatrae* which had guarded the Stainforth Pass that carried a Roman road through the Pennines from Stainmore to Carlisle. As well as an inscribed Roman dedication stone found in the north transept, in the south transept a Saxon font is mounted upon the shaft of a Roman altar. At one time used as tombstone, laying buried for a century or two in the churchyard, the unusual coupling was unearthed a few years ago and brought back inside the church where they stand today.

Rubbing House, Witton Gallops, Middleham High Moor

As the gallops curve round on Middleham High Moor, where countless winners have been trained, there is an unprepossessing derelict stone barn which is actually a legacy of Middleham's horse racing history. This is the Rubbing House, an innovation of the eighteenth century, when it was considered beneficial to wrap a horse up well to make it sweat after training between race day heats, hence the name of this building. The most famous occupant of the Rubbing House was The Flying Dutchman, trained by John Fobert at Spigot Lodge, and winner of the Derby and the St Ledger in 1849 and the Ascot Gold Cup the following year. The practice of 'Yorkshire Sweats' was however a short-lived method of conditioning race horses, and consequently the Rubbing House is a rare survival of its type.

Though breeding and training remain the main industry in the locality today, the tradition far pre-dates the accepted hey-day of the Sport of Kings. In the middle ages the Cistercian monks of Jervaulx bred the finest stallions and destriers (a medieval war horse) in the Dales and probably supplied Middleham Castle. Legend says Richard III's famous destrier White Surrey was bred at Jervaulx, while the White Canons at nearby Coverham Abbey were famed for the magnificent white horses they bred.

The Rubbing House on Witton Gallops, a reminder of Middleham's horse racing and breeding legacy which continues to thrive today

Ruskin's View, Kirkby Lonsdale

From the churchyard of St Mary the Virgin in Kirkby Lonsdale is the vantage point from which Turner painted a view of the River Lune in 1816, inspiring art critic John Ruskin to write: "'*I do not know, in all my own country, still less in France or Italy, a place more naturally divine.*" Signposted from the town, the spot became known as 'Ruskin's View', and remains a draw for lovers of the picturesque today.

This historic market town, where the Dales merge with the Lake District, has a further claim on the curiosity in the unusually named 'Salt Pie Lane'. A short stroll from Ruskin's View, this lane was formerly known as 'Cattle Market Yard', with cattle being sold in the adjoining Horse Market, however an enterprising lady living in the yard exploited the retail advantage of making and selling hot salted mutton pies to the visiting cattle traders, who after nearby Green Dragon Inn to slake their thirst; and the landlord just happened

View from the promontory where 'Ruskin's View' can still be admired

S

Samson's Toe, Langcliffe, Ribblesdale

Of the same ilk as the Norber Erratics (see the letter 'N' for more of these monumental monoliths left behind by the glaciation of the last Ice Age) is 'Samson's Toe', the name given to the large glacial erratic boulder deposited by the receding ice sheet about a mile east of the village of Langcliffe in Ribblesdale. Approximately eight feet high and perched on small eroded limestone plinths at the edge of the scar, this great boulder, supposedly shaped like a giant's big toe, can be found amongst the limestone strewn area of 'Whinskill Rocks', just west of Henside Lane.

As the name suggests, the giant in question is the Biblical Samson, and according to legend he stumbled and lost his footing here while jumping from Langcliffe Scar, breaking off his big toe in the process. Any geological reference book will of course tell you that Samson's Toe was in fact deposited here by the retreating glacial flows moving north-south, the 'toe' perhaps picked up by the glacier somewhere in the Lake District. However the boulder is also known as 'the rocking stone', imbued with the power to grant a wish to anyone strong enough to rock the boulder upon it's pedestal, though you'd need to be as strong as Samson to get his 'toe' to budge even a hair's breadth!

Saxon Cemetery, Masham

In the historic market town of Masham (pronounced 'Massum') in lower Wensleydale the seemingly innocuous installation of new public lavatories in 1988 led to the discovery of a lost Saxon cemetery thought to extend beneath the cobbles of Masham's pair of market squares.

In an earlier less extensive discovery, in the 1930s two skeletons

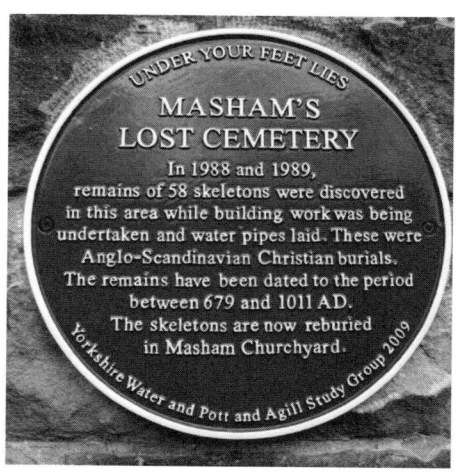

Plaque commemorating Masham's Lost Cemetery

120

were unearthed when a cobbled drainage channel was sunk around the main Market Square, with accounts of further skeletal remains found when footings for the flag pole were dug, and children reportedly seen playing football with a skull! As a precursor to the 1988 discovery, in 1985 work carried out to extend the cellars of the Bruce Arms public house (overlooking Masham's Little Market Place) revealed a portion of what turned out to be significant burial site.

However the real discovery came when water pipes were laid in the vicinity of the Little Market Place. North Yorkshire County Council's Archaeological unit were called in to recover the disturbed human remains, ultimately totalling 58 individuals radiocarbon dating to a burial period between 679 AD to 1011 AD, and indicating a ceme-tery in use for over 300 years. With the odd bone turning up in the flower beds of the gardens of houses bordering on to the Little Market Place, and investigations by 'Dowsers' hinting at further graves beneath the shops facing onto the main Market Square, it is a safe assumption that much of the Saxon cemetery still remains undisturbed, in all probability still holding many further former residents of Masham.

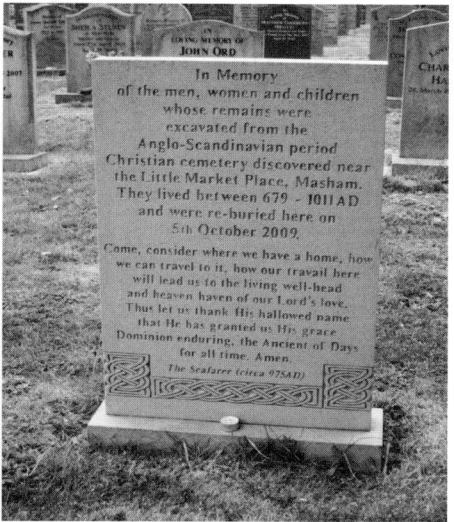

The gravestone in St Mary's churchyard commemorating the reburial of the bones discovered in Masham's lost cemetery

As for the remains, as the original orientation of the graves suggested Christian committal, the bones were reburied in the churchyard of St Mary's in 2009, with the Lord's Prayer read in Anglo-Saxon, Latin and 'Prayer Book English' just to cover all the bases!

Scorton Silver Arrow

Once described as 'The Daddy of all Sporting Fixtures' the annual archery contest for Scorton's Ancient Silver Arrow is the World's longest established and oldest recorded sporting event. The first archery tournament was held on Sunday 14th May 1673 in the village of Scorton, near Richmond, with a view to maintaining the skill of target archery, the practice of which was largely in decline following the English Civil War. Twenty-two archers competed in the first event for the prize of a silver arrow, won by Henry Calverley of Eryholme on Tees who had in fact provided the trophy. The event proved so successful that a new organisation, The Society of Archers, was formed to hold the event on an annual basis.

Open to any Gentleman Archer aged over 21 and shooting with a Longbow or any other 'bare bow' (that is shooting by hand and eye without sights) the competition winner is the first man to hit the three inch centre Black Spot from 100 yards. Named 'Captain of the Arrow', he is presented with a replica of the original silver arrow which he keeps for a year; the original silver arrow held at the Royal Armouries Museum in Leeds.

One of the few sporting fixtures where the competitor is at his own honour to mark his own scorecard, and the convivial consumption of alcohol is permitted on the field of play, there are however prohibitions on unseemly behaviour – cursing is punishable with an on the spot fine of £1, all proceeds of the 'swear bag' given to a local charity. The rules are unclear however when it comes to the 'two-fingered salute', though as the gesture traditionally originated during the Hundred Years War with English archers taunting their French enemies with their bow drawing fingers, perhaps this would be excused!

Scotch Corner, A1 junction with A66

While many, many motorists have driven past this junction over the years, I think few will have paused to consider the reason for its fame and its name, perhaps just grateful not to have been stuck in traffic here… However there are in fact two Scotch Corners in North Yorkshire, and both the sites of battles.

The first, described as 'the modern gateway to Cumbria, the North East and Scotland' is the Scotch Corner on the Great North Road near Richmond, and is one of the best known junctions in the country, the turning point for traffic wishing to go to Scotland, hence the name. Travellers heading for eastern Scotland via the A1 are separated here from those travelling to western Scotland taking the A66, once 'the winter road' from Scotch Corner to Glasgow, by way of Carlisle. 'The summer road' running from Barnard Castle, along Teesdale to Alston, Cumbria, then on to Scotland was particularly favoured by cattle drovers in the past as the route was shorter, when passable.

The first roads to meet at this point were built by the Romans, and the site of the original junction is just a few hundred yards away from the modern day intersection. Scotch Corner also gave its name to the battle fought here in 71 AD when the Romans defeated the Brigantes, a Northern Celtic tribe, who after a number of large battles over the north of England were finally defeated at the Battle of Scotch Corner.

Over the years, the location remained significant as a staging post, subsequently becoming a roadhouse in the early days of motoring with the now iconic Scotch Corner Hotel built on the site of the former sixteenth century inn in 1939.

As to the other and lesser known Scotch Corner, it lies in a quiet location along a track to the southeast of Sutton Bank near Thirsk, just above the village of Oldstead. Less than a mile from the famous Kilburn White Horse and sometimes known as 'Scots Corner' this isolated place was the site of a famous battle also known as The Battle of Scotch Corner. Fought between the Scots and English on 14th October 1322 when England was under attack by Robert Bruce and his army, here the English soldiers, led by the ineffectual King Edward II, lost some 20,000 men, not through fighting, but through disease, hunger and bad management. The king's reputation in ruins, Edward fled south with his tattered troops, and within five years the hapless monarch had been deposed and murdered.

The A1 Southbound approach to Scotch Corner – the weight of traffic on today's busy carriageway a far cry from the stage coaches once plying the Great North Road

Scot Pits Lane, adjacent to site of the Battle of the Standard, near Northallerton

At daybreak on the morning of 22nd August 1138 the Battle of Northallerton, better known as the Battle of the Standard was fought on Cowton Moor, the first major engagement between between the English and the Scots since the Norman Conquest, the consequence of King David I of Scotland monopolising on the civil war endemic in England during the reign of King Stephen.

The result was a resounding victory for the English, the invading Scottish army routed by an army of Yorkshiremen who had gathered on a hill around their standard – a ship's mast mounted on a wagon from which sacred banners flew – hence the Battle's name.

Not long after 9am all the elements of the Scottish army were in retreat or flight, later chroniclers estimating their losses to between ten and twelve thousand, while the English casualty count was relatively light; of the knights present, it is said that only one was killed.

Today a reminder of this bloody engagement still exists in the road called Scot Pits Lane, now a track connecting the Darlington Road out of Northallerton with Brompton Lane. Here in the nineteenth century evidence of mass graves were discovered, with a report from 1891 stating that within living memory '*bones of men and horses have been found...*' confirming the site of the battle and origin of the Lane's name.

A short distance north of Scot Pits Lane there is a battlefield monument set in the layby on the A167 Darlington Road, centered on the point about which the battle was fought almost 900 years ago.

Sedgwick Memorial Fountain, Dent

Adam Sedgwick was born in the lovely Yorkshire Dales village of Dent, or 'Dent Town' as it is known locally, on 22nd March 1785, son of the vicar of St Andrews. This most famous son of the town rose to prominence as an eminent geologist, and building on his illustrious academic achievements, in 1829 Sedgwick was appointed President of the Geological Society of London. It was under Sedgewick that Charles Darwin had studied geology at Cambridge, before departing on the *Beagle* in 1831 as the ship's naturalist. The two men corresponded regularly and Darwin sent many geological specimens back to Sedgwick for examination.

The impressive rough-hewn pink granite memorial to Adam Sedgwick, benefactor of Dent and the town's most famous son

Though Sedgwick was a prominent figure in the arena of Victorian academia, he never lost touch with his roots, and as a mark of recognition to the man who was a great benefactor to the village of his birth, the year after his death, in 1874, the people of Dent erected a memorial fountain in Sedgewick's honour – the impressive rough hewn pink granite monument standing on the corner of Main Street. As a further mark of recognition and to celebrate the bicentenary of Sedgwick's birth, in 1985 a geological trail was created near Dent, The Sedgwick Trail, following the River Clough, highlighting enroute notable rock features and exploring the Dent Fault, a major geological phenomena on the boundary between the counties of Cumbria and North Yorkshire first discover by Sedgwick himself.

Serenading Suicide, Cauldron Snout Waterfall, Middleton-in-Teesdale

Cauldron Snout waterfall, haunt of the Singing Lady

On the upper reaches of the River Tees where the Dales border the Land of the Prince Bishops, immediately below the dam of the Cow Green Reservoir is the imaginatively named Cauldron Snout waterfall. These impressive falls are caused by the upper Tees passing over the dolerite steps of the Whin Sill, creating a tumultuous cascade of over a 200 yard rock 'stairway'. It was here at the head of the falls that an unfortunate Victorian farm girl took her own life in desolation and despair after her love affair with a local lead miner ended. As a consequence the haunting melodies of the 'Singing Lady' have been heard on cold moonlit nights, and it is said that the wraith of a sad young woman sits on the rocks near the Snout and sings of the loss of her love.

Sharow Sanctuary Cross, Sharow, Ripon

In the middles ages the right to sanctuary was often the only recourse for fugitives fleeing the law, and while it was usually sought inside a church (or by laying hold of the sanctuary ring affixed to many church doors) some entire towns were granted sanctuary status, within the boundary of which an accused wrongdoer could remain immune from prosecution.

The City of Ripon is one such example, as in 937 AD King Athelstan granted the right of sanctuary as part of The Liberty of St Wilfrid. The sanctuary boundary, within

The Sharow Cross, the only survivor of the eight original crosses marking the limits of Ripon's "sanctuary"

which anyone would be granted protection overnight was originally marked by eight stone crosses, each one placed at a one mile radius from the cathedral. The last surviving of these crosses, the Sharow Cross, can be seen at the junction of Sharow Lane and Dishforth Road in the village of Sharow (pronounced 'share-ah'), one mile as the crow flies from the Cathedral, and marking the north-eastern limits of the sanctuary. However in 2005, to mark the centenary celebration of Rotary International, the Ripon chapter setup replica sanctuary stones close to the sites of the originals denoting Ripon's original sanctified boundary, linking them in a fascinating circular walk around the City.

Slavering Sal, East Witton, Wensleydale

In woods on the southern reaches of the lovely Dales village of East Witton lays hidden Slavering (or Slobbering) Sal, an ancient spring emerging from a grotesque stone head, hence her salivating soubriquet. Sal waters at the mouth into a stone basin, close to the grotto housing Diana's Well, the original water supply for the village, the well retaining its Roman connection and never Christianised. The inscription on the arched entrance to the grotto: '*Mqfs of A 1821*' is a reference to the Earl of Aylesbury who at one time lived at nearby Jervaulx Abbey and had the grotto built as a picnicking venue for his friends and family, complete with a large stone slab for a table.

There was an old rhyme repeated hereabouts associated with the well that ran:

> *Whoever eats Hammer Nuts and drinks Diana's water*
> *Will never leave Witton Town while he's rag or tatter.*

The elements of these prophetic lines allude to the hazelnuts that used to grow in Hammer Woods which surround the well dedicated to Diana, the Roman Goddess of the moon, and Witton folk's proverbial attachment to the place.

Another name for this well is the 'Castaway Well' (the forest track leading to the well is called 'Castaway Ride') the name according to tradition deriving from the practice of throwing an offering into the well waters, and here specifically pins were cast in for good luck and the granting of wishes.

Somnolent Skull, Kirkby Malzeard

In the days when many matters now regarded as the province of the secular authorities would have been heard before a Church Court, records from the seventeenth century show that ecclesiastic judgement could be severe on even the mere suspicion of a variety of crimes; the sheltering of unmarried mothers, offering refuge to Catholics, adultery and fornication to name but a few. Hearings of such Church Courts were regularly held to discuss village as well as church matters, and in St Andrew's at Kirkby Malzeard, in 1640 Marmaduke Loftus was excommunicated for '*making water against the churchyard*'! However, the trial conducted there in 1639 of one Janet Burniston concerned the charge of taking a skull from the churchyard. In her defense, Janet

claimed that she was merely assisting a fellow parishioner, Christopher Head, who was suffering chronic insomnia, and sited the belief that the placing of a human skull beneath the sufferer's pillow was a powerful charm against sleeplessness.

In this instance Janet was fortunate to be dismissed with a reprimand and an order to return the skull to the churchyard. The death penalty for witchcraft remained on the statue books until the passing of the Witchcraft Act in 1735, the last execution for witchcraft in England taking place in 1716 when Mary Hicks and her nine year old daughter Elizabeth were hung in Huntingdon.

Within St Andrew's churchyard there is also the curiously named 'witchcraft corner', and presumably related to Janet Burneston and her cranial caper...

Stanwick Fortifications, Stanwick St John, near Scotch Corner

Also known as 'Stanwick Camp' the system of Iron Age ditches and ramparts still completely surround the village of Stanwick St John today. One of the largest Iron Age settlements in Britain (in extent if not necessarily in population), Stanwick was excavated by Sir Mortimer Wheeler over the summers of 1951-52 as one of his last major archaeological investigations.

Wheeler concluded that Stanwick had been the rebel stronghold of Venutius, who had separated from his wife, the pro-Roman Brigantian queen Cartimandua after she had taken his charioteer and armour-bearer Vellocatus as a lover, as well as betraying Venutius's fellow rebel leader Caractacus to the Romans. Mooted as the location where Venutius had rallied his anti-Roman Brigante tribesmen in revolt against the Roman invaders, finds at Stanwick included an Iron Age sword, unusually still well-preserved in its ash wood scabbard, and nearby the skull of a severed head was found exhibiting the savage marks of wounds inflicted by an axe or a sword. These finds, located close to the main north- western gate, led to Wheeler's further supposition that the severed head may once have been hung from the gate as a trophy or a grim warning to enemies. Grisly connotations aside, sections of Stanwick's 2,000 year old fortifications make for an interesting and enjoyable walk.

Stepping Stones

Probably the earliest form of river crossing before the construction of span bridges, some picturesque examples still exist in the Dales, and the riverside village of Gargrave boasts not one but two sets of 'Buttertub' style stepping-stones. Though Gargrave is blessed with a sturdy stone bridge crossing the River Aire, the stepping stones connecting Water Street and High Green and those crossing the river between Middle Green and Low Green are a draw for paddling children in the summer months.

A wider challenge, there are 57 stepping stones crossing the River Wharfe at Bolton Abbey. Founded in 1154 by the Augustinian order, Bolton Abbey was

The Abbey Stepping Stones crossing the River Wharfe at Bolton Priory (courtesy of Snapshots Of The Past)

technically a Priory despite its name. In its monastic heyday the stepping stones on the old right of way linking the hamlet of Storiths with the Priory were the only way to cross the river without getting your feet wet. Today the stepping stones over the Wharfe are a source of fun and adventure for both children and adults alike, though for the not so daring there is an adjacent footbridge.

Another fine set of much photographed ancient stepping stones again cross the River Wharfe as it skirts the peaceful churchyard of St Michael & All Angels, downstream from Linton Falls where the waters cascades through a series of channels formed by a discontinuity in the limestone bedrock. It is said that the environs of St Michael's are haunted by the spirit of a wandering monk, perhaps accounting for the heavy phantom footsteps that have been heard along the riverside walk at Linton, however if the ghostly brother had a mind to cross the river, there are no less than three stone bridges in the village ensuring that his spectral sandals won't get wet!

Strid, River Wharfe, near Bolton Abbey

To the north of Bolton Bridge, on the Bolton Abbey estate, The Strid is the name given to a notorious stretch of water where the River Wharfe is forced through a deep, narrow gorge holding a dark reputation, as here where the channel diminishes to its point, a mere two meters in width, the foolhardy are often tempted to jump. The width of the gap looks a deceptively easy leap but the varying heights of the rock ledges on either side, which are often very slippery, have given rise to the saying that 'nobody ever fails to jump the Strid *twice*', as one false step invariable proves fatal. Wordsworth was clearly aware of the Strid's reputation as in his poem *The Founding Of Bolton Priory*, one of the verses alludes to the drowning of the 'Boy of Egremont', who was foolish enough to attempt the jump...

> *"The boy is in the arms of Wharf,*
> *And strangled by a merciless force;*
> *For never more was young Romilly seen*
> *Till he rose a lifeless corse"*

('Corse' is an archaic form of corpse or dead body.)

Though the Strid is a tempestuous and wonderful sight, as the safety notices attest maintaining a safe distance is advisable. Beneath the churning surface of the powerful currents running through this turbulent channel lie hidden underwater caves and eroded chambers, the haunts of a malevolent pale horse, a fairy steed, said to rise from the foam of the Strid every May Day morning. While accounts vary, the phantom palid palfrey is usually accompanied by a fairy who promises to grant any eager human a wish, and tell their fortune into the bargain. But these promises belie a sinister reputation as both horse and fairy are said to appear before the imminent drowning of anyone in the Strid, their annual intent to fatally immerse those incautious enough to venture too close to the rapids. This was the fate that befell three sisters, the co-heiresses of Beamsley Hall on the edge of the Bolton Abbey estate, who many years ago thought they'd try their luck one May Day morning. Whether or not their ultimate fates were revealed to them before they drowned, their bodies were later recovered washed further downstream.

In 1843, Airedale Poet John Nicholson penned *Lines on the young lady who drowned in the Strid* alluding to a further tragedy in the watery demise of 'young Eliza'. Sadly the fierce running waters of the Strid have continued to claim numerous lives since, the lines of this old rhyme still ringing true today:

'Wharfe is clear, and Aire is lithe;
Where Aire kills one, Wharfe kills five'

The tempestuous channel of The Strid

T

Temple Folly, Swinithwaite, Wensleydale

Now beautifully restored from a ruinous state into a weekend hideaway, with a balconied turret bedroom much favoured by honeymooning couples, the octagonal gothic Temple Folly was the former hunting lodge built in the eighteenth century for the the Swinithwaite Estate. Sheltered from the rumbling traffic on the road to Aysgarth by a high wall, the northern aspect holds splendid views out across the River Ure toward Bolton Castle.

Temple Folly was so named as the secluded woodland setting is a stone's throw from the ruined twelfth century Knights Templar Preceptory mentioned under the letter 'K'. Built in 1792 as a hunting lodge and sometime summer house for the then owner of Swinithwaite Hall just a mile down the road, it is said that Temple Folly is frequented by the benign ghost of a jolly looking huntsman who has appeared to several guest over the years, usually just inside the bedroom door around midnight. Dressed in hunting pink, it is assumed that he is one of the Anderson family who built Swinithwaite Hall 1767.

Thief Hole Lane, Thornton-le-Moor, near Northallerton

The imaginatively named Thief Hole Lane branches off from the A168 Northallerton road towards Thornton-le-Moor, the largest village in the parish, about a mile south of the pleasingly named Thornton-le-Beans. Local folklore tells of how, many centuries ago, highwaymen would hide in a large hole at the end of the lane, ready to rob the occupants of the passing coaches travelling the main London-Edinburgh road, hence the Lane's name. However much truth can be attributed to the tradition, Thief Hole has certainly been known by this name since 1657 when it was noted that the way over 'Purgatory' by Thief Hole Lane was in want of repair, 'Purgatory' being the name given to the southeast corner of the parish east of the road, and not a reference to the still prevalent state of North Yorkshire's roads! Thankfully a toll is no longer payable at Purgatory Bar, long since vanished, along with the highwaymen.

Thomas Lord's House, Thirsk

In the old fashioned market town of Thirsk, famed as James Herriot's 'Darrowby', almost directly across the road from 'The World of James Herriot'

131

museum on Kirkgate is an unobtrusive building where Thomas Lord was born in 1755. Famous as the founder of Lord's Cricket Ground in London, Lord's house is now home to the Thirsk Museum, with exhibits of local history and as one would expect, cricket ephemera. Also on display in the museum, but suspended from a strong hook high up on the wall is the 'Busby Stoop Chair' – a full explanation of this elevated exhibit can be found in the Chair's entry under the letter 'B'.

Thornborough Henge, outskirts of Thornborough Village, near West Tanfield

While Neolithic Earthworks are not a common feature in the Dales landscape, when it comes to Thornborough Henge one could argue that the old adage 'quality not quantity' certainly applies. A complex of three aligned henges, close to the village of the same name, this extensive group of cursus, henges and burial grounds have been credited by English Heritage as the most important ancient site between

Thomas Lord's birthplace, now home to Thirsk Museum

Stonehenge in Wiltshire and Skara Brae on Orkney, this collectively sizeable feature often described as 'The Stonehenge of the North'.

The revival of the celebration of the ancient Gaelic May Day festival of Beltane is now in its tenth year at Thornborough, drawing revellers from far and wide to the central henge, keeping alive the tradition of marking the transition of winter into summer with the burning of a wicker man, fire being a key part of the festival, and continuing the use of this ritual landscape thousands of years on from its original ceremonial beginnings.

Thornthwaite Packhorse Bridge, Thornthwaite with Padside, near Pateley Bridge

A rare survivor of its kind and effectively unaltered, this quaint single arched stone bridge crossing the Padside Beck was once on the monks' route between the Cistercian abbey at Fountains and the Augustinian Bolton Abbey. Lining up with the old tracks radiating from Fountains, the path north-east from the bridge runs along Monk Ing Road towards the old river crossing at Summerbridge.

In medieval times both abbeys owned great estates in Wharfedale and their monks evolved networks of roads and green lanes to travel between them; one such drove road called Mastiles Lane above Kilnsey Crag can still be walked today – see the Lane's entry under the letter 'M'.

Tom Taylor's Tunnel, How Stean Gorge, Nidderdale

Thornthwaite's picturesque and today seldom crossed Packhorse Bridge

How Stean Gorge itself is something of a curiosity, with mazes of footpaths and wobbly bridges, here caves and potholes have been hollowed out of the limestone rock by the constant flow of water over thousands of years. There are also many tales and legends about the Gorge, one of which concerns Tom Taylor, highway and robber renowned for his cruelty and indiscriminate selection of victims, often killing unfortunate travellers in cold blood before making off with his ill-gotten gains. Starting out as part of a gang specialising in robbing isolated farmsteads, Tom branched out on his own to pursue a more lucrative career in highway robbery, with his secret lair in the now infamous cave in How Stean

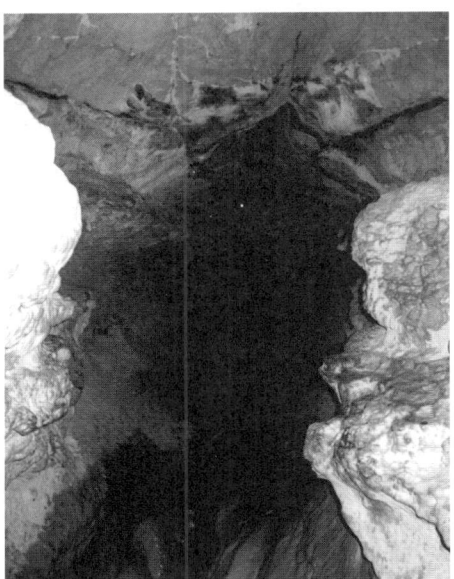

Tom Taylor's cave hideout, How Stean Gorge, Nidderdale

Gorge known as 'Tom Taylor's Tunnel'. Accessing his hideaway by scaling the rocks at the side of the Gorge or scrambling through a hidden entrance concealed by tree roots, Tom's secret cave is now a popular feature of How

Stean, which first became a tourist attraction in the Victorian era with a gala opening on 18th August 1869, admission one shilling to include tea and a brass band performance.

Today's visitors to the Gorge are offered the option of a torch on entrance, for a minimal charge, which is a must if one is to fully appreciate the amazing cavern where Tom Taylor would hide and count his money. We must assume that the locals who finally caught up with Tom and hung him from the metal bar still apparent in the roof of the Beehive Chamber were equally well illuminated, and the rough justice meted out by them giving rise to the tales of Tom Taylor's ghost still haunting the cave...

Tor Dyke, valley head between Coverdale and Upper Wharfedale

The tangible remains of the Brigantes tribal resistance to the Roman occupation of the north of England can still be seen in the landscape today in the form of of an extensive ditch known as 'Tor Dyke', the earthworks forming a defensive trench close to Great Whernside. Cut by the the valley road that steeply descends on its approach to Kettlewell, the man-made linear fortification, linking in with the natural escarpment, stretches for some three miles across the valley head and once guarded access from Upper Wharfedale into Coverdale. Doubtless this spot would have seen many engagements and skirmishes between Venutius's Celts and the invading Romans; there are several ancient yet artificial mounds scattered about this part of North Moor suggesting the burial sites of the fallen Brigantes tribesmen slain in battle nearly a thousand years ago, and giving rise to local legends of the restless spirits of slain warriors still haunting their old battle ground. After the the Empire's eventual withdrawal from Northern and Western Britain in the late fourth century AD, Tor Dyke became the north-eastern boundary of the Dark Age kingdom of Craven and once again formed a defensive frontline against Anglian invaders keen to encroach on northern native territories.

The sloping edge of the ancient valleyhead fortification of Tor Dyke, interrupted by the road as it leaves the lonely expanse of North Moor to drop down Park Rash, an extraordinary descent with some sharp bends but affording splendid views of Upper Wharfedale

Just half a mile from Tor Dyke on the lonely road crossing North Moor heading for Horsehouse is another Curiosity of note – The Hunter's Stone. For more of this mystery monolith said to spin at midnight in the shadow of Great Whernside, see the Stone's entry under the letter 'H'.

Troller's Gill, Appletreewick, Wharfedale

Troller's Gill is the sinister limestone gorge near Appletreewick noted as the haunt of Scandinavian trolls, sprites and flesh eating boggarts, they liking nothing better than to roll rocks down on to the heads of any unsuspecting souls entering their ravine. Troller's Gill is also home to the Dale's fiercest breed of Barguest, those baleful black phantom dogs detailed under the letter 'B'.

Almost a thousand feet long, this popular walking route cuts deep into the limestone of Great Scar ending close to Gill Heads where the remains of an abandoned lead mine can be found. In Parkinson's *Yorkshire Legends & Traditions* (1888) the huge and fearsome long haired Barguest haunting this ravine has eyes the size of saucers and razor sharp saliva flecked teeth, though this account did nothing to deter an intrepid local man intent on witnessing the beast for himself. Setting off one windy moonlit evening, descending into the lonely and foreboding fissure intending to spend the night, despite taking the superstitious precaution of remaining within a circle drawn on the ground and thrice kissing the damp soil on which he stood, on his challenging summoning of the beast, a howling wind blew up:

> *'And a dreadful thing from the cliff did spring;*
> *Its wild bark thrilled around;*
>
> *And a fiendish glow flashed forth I trow,*
> *From the eyes of the Spectre Hound. '*

Unfortunately, for our dauntless Barguest spotter the protective magic employed had no power to repel this particular Hell Hound, and his body, later discovered by a shepherd the following morning was said to exhibit wounds and marks not possibly inflicted by the hand of man...

As well as the obvious potential for meeting a sticky end (assuming of course that you manage to avoid all the trolls and boggarts hurling rocks at you) an encounter with the Troller's Gill Barguest – which incidentally happens to be the size of a small bear – should on no account involve staring into his flaming yellow saucer sized eyes, as to do so would result in calamity within a few days, a trait shared with many of the ghostly hounds regarded as a harbinger of doom throughout the Dales...

U

Ulshaw Bridge Sundial, Lower Wensleydale

Two miles to the southeast of Middleham, childhood home of Richard III, the ancient road from Richmond and the North cross over into Coverdale via the triple arched Ulshaw Bridge spanning the River Ure. There has been a crossing point at Ulshaw for at least 2,000 years as here the Roman road from Swaledale met the river, and by the medieval period Ulshaw Bridge was the primary crossing point over the Ure, lying close to the military and political stronghold of the aforementioned military Middleham Castle and Jervaulx Abbey to the south east.

The Ulshaw Bridge sundial

However, the real curiosity here is sheltered in one of of the bridge's mid-span pedestrian refuges – on the upstream side is a lovely old octagonal sundial plinth inscribed 'R W 1674'. Missing its dial and gnomon, it is somewhat redundant in telling the time, and as there are no records verifying by whom, when or why it was placed here, something of a timeless mystery.

Unidentified Commemorative Fountain, Masham

In 1887 Queen Victoria celebrated her Golden Jubilee. There were celebrations all over the country, and in common with many towns and villages the good people of Masham raised funds to erect a commemorative fountain to mark their monarch's 50 years on the throne.

In that year, on 23rd June after the ceremonial laying of the fountain's foundation stone, an official procession made its way to Masham Market Place. Almost every hamlet and village in the district was represented, and men, women and children cheered loudly as the throng passed along Silver Street accompanied by a brass band and the peal of St Mary's church bells.

However, with the outbreak of World War II, precautionary measures in case of German invasion meant that many road signs and place names countrywide were either painted over or removed, the better to hinder Hitler's progress. Though the Nazi invasion plan, Operation Sea Lion, was never taken beyond the preliminary assembly of forces, to this day one can still see where the words 'of Mashamshire' have been scoured from the surface of the stone inscription carved on the commemorative plaque backing the Jubilee Fountain.

Masham's unidentified commemorative fountain

Upsall Castle, near Thirsk
The fourteenth century ruins of Upsall Castle, 'slighted' during the English Civil War are associated with two curious strands of folklore, one concerning buried treasure and the second pertaining to a curse...

Many, many years ago there lived in Upsall village a man called Jack who dreamed, on three successive nights, that if he travelled south to London Bridge he would hear something greatly to his advantage. Nagged by the theme of his recurrent dreams, Jack walked the entire distance from Upsall to London, and on arrival in the Capital he headed straight for London Bridge, where he waited day in, day out until his patience had all but deserted him.

On the point of returning home, thinking he had embarked on a fool's errand, Jack was approached by a Quaker who politely enquired why he had been camped out on the bridge for so long. After reluctantly admitting to his fantastical dreams, the Quaker laughed and himself confided to having had the self same dream the night before, but in his sleep he had been directed to go to Upsall in North Yorkshire, a place he didn't know, and to dig under a certain bush in the grounds of the castle where upon he would find a pot of gold.

Noting Jack's Yorkshire accent, the Quaker enquired whether he knew where Upsall was, however Jack astutely pleaded ignorance and immediately set off home in search of the Quaker's dream horde. After digging beneath a likely looking bush, Jack unearthed a pot filled with gold, covered with a lid on which was written an inscription in a language he did not understand. The gold went straight into Jack's pocket, while the pot and cover were preserved as a memento in the village inn, where one day a bearded stranger, looking not unlike a Jew, caught sight of the pot and translated the inscription from the lid:

> Look lower where this stood
> Is another twice as good

On hearing the pot's message in plain English, Jack resumed his spade work, returning to the bush and digging deeper he found another pot filled with gold and far more valuable than the first. Encouraged by this good fortune Jack dug deeper still and found yet another pot containing treasure of even greater value. The moral of this story – good things come to those who wait – and dig!

Less benign than the tale of hidden gold, which incidentally may have been 'borrowed' from the Persian story *One Thousand and One Nights*, is the tradition of the Upsall Curse...

Sir John Constable, who was lord of Upsall Castle at the time of the Civil War was a strong supporter of the Royalist cause. As mentioned earlier, Upsall was 'slighted' by the Parliamentarians, a fate which befell many castles and fortified houses, rendering them useless to the enemy. By the time of Charles II's Restoration in 1660, Upsall had fallen into complete ruin, yet Sir John had remained steadfast to the Crown throughout the Commonwealth years, and he is said to have uttered a curse on any succeeding owner of Upsall who should prove disloyal to his king and country.

Upside Down Waterfall, Cray, Langstrothdale

The splendid landscape surrounding the tiny hamlet of Cray in Upper Wharfedale, nestling beneath Buckden Pike and consisting of a very few scattered farms and a pub, the White Lion Inn, is renowned for a series of several attractive cascades known collectively as Cray Waterfalls.

A little further downstream from the The White Lion Inn, where the rushing Cray Gill plummets over a limestone scar before joining the waters of the River Wharfe below, a curious phenomenon has been observed, as when the prevailing wind blows a stiff south-westerly the waterfall appears to flow upside down!

Uther Pendragon

The now ruined Pendragon Castle near the hamlet of Outhgill in remote Mallerstang Dale reputedly stands on the site of an earlier castle, built some 600 years previously by Uther Pendragon, father of the legendary King Arthur. A fifth century chieftain who led local resistance against the invading Anglo-Saxons, Uther has attracted much folklore and legend over time, with tales of how he battled a large dragon-like serpent while in Mallerstang, and his attempts to reroute the River Eden to create a moat around Pendragon Castle. According to tradition it was at Pendragon that Uther met his end, he and a hundred of his men killed within the castle when Saxon invaders infiltrated the fortress after poisoning the waters of the castle well. While the existing ruins of the Norman castle date to the twelfth century, the legends of Uther's ghost still hold, as do the tales of the hoard of treasure hidden therein, but protected by a phantom black hen! For more of this plucky pecking guardian see the letter 'X'.

Howard Pyle's illustration of Uther Pendragon from the 1903 edition of The Story of King Arthur and His Knights

V

Valley Of Desolation, Wharfedale

This dramatically named valley, about a mile north of the village of Bolton Abbey on the Chatsworth Estate, belonging to the Duke and Duchess of Devonshire, was so named after the scene of desolation following the great storm which raged over Barden Fell in 1836. Strong winds, torrential rain and flash floods produced a storm surge from Posforth Gill uprooting most of the trees in the area.

While a few decaying oaks and rotting logs are obvious reminders of this once richly wooded valley, over the passing years the signs of damage have gradually disappeared as natural regeneration and regrowth has occurred, assisted by the planting of eight thousand new trees in 1999. The legacy of the decimation wrought by Mother Nature is however perpetuated in the Valley's name.

Vampire of Dent

There is a legend that the folk of Dent are fond of telling, of a resident vampire who is still buried beneath a stone slab in front of the porch of St Andrew's Church. The vampire, George Hodgson, was a man well into his nineties when he died in 1715, though he was noted for a remarkable sprightliness in one so old, the townsfolk attributing this to a pact that George was said to have made with the Devil. His active longevity coupled with his enjoyment of a daily glass of sheep's blood as a tonic and the curious shape of his teeth was enough to convince his neighbours that George was in fact a vampire, their suppositions further reinforced when George's corpse was seen in and around Dent long after his burial, and those claiming to have seen the resurrected George suffering a swift demise. By popular demand an exhumation was ordered, and when the coffin was opened it was observed that George's pallor was still pink and healthy and that his hair and nails had continued to grow. Hastily re-buried beneath a stone slab in front of the church

George Hodgson's grave at the entrance to St Andrew's Church, Dent. The Vampiric safeguarding measure is still apparent!

door, as a final precaution a hole was made in the tombstone through which a brass stake was driven into the heart of George's corpse; you can still see the hole and the top of the shorn off stake today, although the sceptical maintain that the burial slab is merely a re-used gatepost...

Victoria Cave, Settle

One of several caves in the district where the remains of prehistoric inhabitants have been found, Victoria Cave was so named as it was discovered in on 20th June 1837, the day Queen Victoria acceded to the throne.

As the mouth of the cave was blocked by large stones, it was a man named Michael Horner who accidentally discovered the main chamber when his dog chasing a rabbit entered a small opening and reappeared out of another. Removing debris and some of the smaller boulders Horner crawled inside, there finding coins in the topsoil from the Romano British period. Later a full scale excavation revealed a cave consisting of four chambers, one of them about 120 feet by 30 feet but very low, and another inner chamber where the remains of reindeer, mammoth and hippopotamus were discovered along with a bear's skull, a worked flint and a harpoon head carved from antler.

Designated a Scheduled Monument and a Site of Special Scientific Interest, the cave and the surrounding scar are now owned and looked after by the Yorkshire Dales National Park Authority, having been purchased by the West Riding County Council in 1972 to protect the cave and to secure public access. The cave is still open, though visitors are not encouraged to go beyond the safety barriers inside, however there is a 'Victoria Cave Revisited' exhibition at The Museum of North Craven Life in Settle celebrating the cave's discovery, and where the Victorian archaeological finds are also on display.

Victorian Lamp Post, Victoria Grove, Ripon

Said to be the last of its type in the whole of the Harrogate district, this lamp post is an illuminating vestige of Ripon's Victorian past and a testament to the ingenuity of that era as originally it was methane gas from the city's sewers that was harnessed to provide street lighting for Ripon.

Though coming close to being removed, the lamp post was saved and refurbished by the Ripon Civic Society and still lights Victoria Grove today, re-connected however to the city's main gas supply and no longer dependent on the miasmas of Ripon's Victorian drains!

Viking Vestiges

When the initial wave of Danish raiders hit the coastline of the British Isles their first attack is believed to have taken place on 2nd February 793 when the Nordic raiders destroyed the church at Lindisfarne. However, by 835 the Viking invasion had begun in earnest, and in 867 the Kingdom of Northumbria was replaced by the Viking Kingdom of York (Jorvik), the north eastern half of England settled by the newcomers and under the influence of the 'Danelaw' by the 890s.

As well as the many local place names with Norse derivations such as Thorpe, Cracoe and Skyreholme telling us that the Vikings settled in and around the Wharfe Valley over a thousand years ago, tangible evidence of the Viking incursions and later settlement of this part North Yorkshire can be found at St Wilfrid's Church in Burnsall. Here a unique collection of stone sculptures including Viking 'Hogback' tombstones and fragments of Anglo-Scandinavian crosses dating from the ninth to the eleventh centuries now form an exhibition aimed at unravelling Burnsall's rich Viking past. Discovered beneath the floor of the church by workmen carrying out building repairs during the nineteenth century, on display are three of the curved shaped ridged backed tombs symbolic of the stylised 'houses' intended for the dead, and a funerary monument favoured by the Scandinavian settlers who occupied Northern England.

The Viking stonework on display in St Wilfrid's may well have been influenced by the collection of Hogback tombs now on show in St Thomas' Church at Brompton-in-Allertonshire. Reputed to be the largest collection of Hogback sculptures in the United Kingdom, it has been suggested that Brompton was the base for a company of stone carvers during the nineth century, leading to the supposition that the Hogback was in fact invented in the Allertonshire area, as here we find the oldest examples. Incorporating a variety of carved decorative patterns, including interlacing knotwork with terminals representing playful

Exhibition of Burnsall's Viking past in St Wilfrid's Church

muzzled bears, a combination of English and Scandinavian influences, both the collections at Brompton and Burnsall are well worth a visit.

Village Lock-Up, North Stainley, near Ripon

Convenient for the temporary detention of miscreants in those rural areas removed from the more capacious holding facilities of larger towns and cities, village 'lock-ups' were often used to temporarily hold people being brought before the local magistrate, or drunkards who were usually released the following day after sober reflection in what was usually a confined and miserable space.

Typically small, free standing structures with a single door and a narrow slit window or opening, most lock-ups feature a spire shaped roof, as does the example still standing opposite the Stavely Arms pub in North Stainley. While it has been suggested that this lock-up is in fact a decorative Gazebo built for the Staveley family of nearby Stainley Hall, whatever the buildings original intended use, in view of its proximity to the Stavely Arms and to a private house that was once the Cross Keys Inn, I think that Stainley's lock-up may well have been utilised as a rustic 'drunk tank' in days gone by...

Former village lock-up at North Stainley, opposite The Staveley Arms pub

Vincenz's Bath, Ilkley

The Victorian architecture and wide streets of Ilkley are a vestige of the town's rise to prominence as a spa resort, thanks to the discovery of the healing powers of the ice-cold waters of the moorland spring at White Wells. Based on the ideas of Vincenz Priessnitz, a Silesian farmer who introduced the world

The Ben Rhydding Hydro c. 1858, the fountain honouring Vincenz Priessnitz is shown in the foreground far right

to the idea that water, so long as it was cold enough, could cure all kinds of ailments, the early Victorians enthusiastically embraced the idea of hydropathic treatment.

In 1843, a merchant called Hamer Stansfield set up a company to build Britain's first Hydro at Ben Rhydding close to Ilkley, akin to the establishments we know today as health farms. In the grounds of the Hydro a temple was built to Vincenz Priessnitz, including a fountain, honouring his discovery. While the Ben Rhydding Hydro has long since been demolished, a bath which was was once part of the Priessnitz temple now stands in a small garden on The Grove, Ilkley's principal shopping street, inscribed to '*The Silesian peasant to whom the world is indebted for the blessing of the SYSTEM OF CURE BY COLD WATER*'.

Virgin's Crown, St Mary's Church, Alne

In days gone by, funeral processions for unmarried young girls were often headed by a friend or family member carrying a 'Virgin's Crown'. Usually made of light wood and embellished with strips of white linen or paper, these crowns were symbolic of the deceased's purity. Later hung inside the church, usually above the pew where the girl had worshipped, a

A rare and poignant reminder of the old custom attending the burial of unmarried girls is preserved in St Mary's Church, Alne

rare example is still displayed (now in a protective perspex case) at St Mary's Church, Alne.

This touching practice was common in England, Wales and Scotland before the Reformation and though the tradition continued for some two hundred years or more thereafter, the Virgin's Crown in Alne church dated 1709 is a rare survivor.

Viscountess buried at sea, St Cuthbert and St Oswald, Winksley, near Ripon

In the church of St Cuthbert and St Oswald there is the beautiful marble monument in memory of Daisy, wife of Marmaduke Viscount Furness of Grantley, buried at sea on 25th February 1921 off the coast of Portugal.

Ada 'Daisy' Hogg had married the Right Honourable Marmaduke Furness in 1904, becoming Lady Furness when her husband inherited his father's title in 1912. Lady Daisy, who had been active as a Red Cross nurse during the First World War, was en route by sea with her husband to join her children and her mother-in-law in the South of France. Having undergone a serious operation at the end of 1920, she suffered a sudden relapse and died, aged 40, onboard the Viscount's steam-powered yacht, the 'Sapphire'. Buried at sea off Cadiz, Daisy's memorial was placed in Winksley church, close to the family seat at Grantley Hall, amongst the monuments and resting places of other members of the Furness family.

W

Wakeman's Ceremony, Ripon

On the south side of Ripon's marketplace, on the facade of the Georgian Town Hall is the inscription: '*Except Ye Lord keep Ye Cittie, Ye Wakeman Waketh in Vain*'. Pertaining to the old custom of 'setting the night watch' at the four corners of the obelisk in the Market Square, at 9pm every evening the unbroken 1,000 year old tradition is still performed. Originally charged with the task of warning the populace of any impending peril by sounding the 'Wakeman's Horn', the incumbent Wakeman, in full regalia, still blows on the instrument every evening, his blasts coinciding with the ringing of the curfew bell from the tower of Ripon Cathedral.

The office of Ripon's Wakeman became that of Mayor in 1604, and in the sixteenth century Mayor's House, a rare surviving example of early timber-framed construction, the white clad ghost of Hugh Ripley, the City's most famous Wakeman and first Lord Mayor has been seen to appear at the upper windows. Generations of the Precious family who occupied the Mayor's House for nearly a century from the 1820s were often woken by Hugh's footsteps, his spectre often seen making an appearance in one of the front bedroom windows; perhaps just making sure his horn was still being blown...

The facade of Ripon's Georgian Town Hall bearing the inscription 'Except Ye Lord keep Ye Cittie, Ye Wakeman Waketh in Vain'

Watery Grave, churchyard of St Michael the Archangel, Kirkby Malham

In the northwest part of the churchyard of the austerely beautiful fifteenth century St Michaels, whose bells are incidentally those heard by 'Tom' in Charles Kingsley's *Water Babies*, is the unusual resting place of Colonel and

Mrs Harrison. Colonel Harrison was often unavoidably separated from his wife Helen for extended periods while serving overseas, and it was she who vowed '*as water parted us in life, so it shall in death.*' As a literal interpretation, Mrs Harrison made arrangements that a small stream should be routed to flow through their grave plot, however the local geology conspired to prevent her final wishes being carried out. On her death in 1890 Mrs Harrison was buried in the plot to the south side of the stream, but on the death of Colonel Harrison ten years later it was found on digging his grave that the north side of the burial plot was rendered impenet-rable by solid rock. Though the couple were ultimately interred together, their memorial nonethe-less does straddle the small stream.

The Watery Grave in the churchyard of St Michael the Archangel

Weeping Cross, Ripley, near Harrogate

In the churchyard of All Saints Church, Ripley there is the base of an unusual Medieval stone cross, thought to be the only surviving example of a Weeping Cross in the country.

Surrounding the base are eight recesses, where the knees or perhaps the heads of the Penitent rested as they prayed for absolution. While the exact age of the cross in unknown, it is certainly as old as the church which was built in the fourteenth century (a contemporary

Ripley's Weeping Cross, complete with carved niches for penitent knees

147

of the nearby Ripley Castle), the cross may have been connected to an earlier chapel on the site, known as the Sinking Chapel as the original church here become ruinous because of its proximity to the Ripley Beck.

Though All Saints Church remains buoyant, it does bear the scars of a violent past as along one of its walls Cromwell's Parliamentarian soldiers lined up and executed Royalist prisoners taken after the battle of Marston Moor fought on 2nd July 1644; the bullet holes still visible today.

White Boar or Warwick's Bear?
Middleham

Known as the 'Windsor of the North' in view of the magnificence of Middleham Castle boasting the largest keep in the north of England, though the once great fortress is now in ruins, the childhood home of King Richard III still dominates the busy little market town today.

Clusters of old grey stone cottages and fine Georgian and Victorian houses look out upon the town's two cobbled squares, the lower and larger market square dominated by a tall Medieval cross, while the upper square, or Swine Market is centred around the less substantial remains of another fifteenth century market cross, next to which is the worn effigy of a reclining animal.

Though this timeworn creature has been weathered almost beyond recognition, it is a safe supposition that it might well have been a representation of Richard III's heraldic emblem – a white boar, erected to commemorate a grant obtained by Richard (then Duke of Gloucester) in 1479 for Middleham to hold a twice yearly fair and market. However, it is equally plausible that this battered beast is a bear, the personal device of the Earls of Warwick, as Middleham Castle was the favourite residence of Richard Neville, Earl of Warwick, who was in possession of Middleham when his young cousin Richard of Gloucester came there to learn the skills of knighthood in 1462. After the death of the 'Kingmaker' at the Battle of Barnet in 1471, Richard became master of Middleham Castle and the following year married Warwick's daughter, Anne Neville. It was at Middleham in the round tower at the south-west corner of the curtain wall, traditionally known as the Prince's Tower, that their only child Edward was born in December 1473, and there sadly died on 31st March 1484 before reaching his eleventh birthday.

Middleham does have one further claim on the letter W's curiosities in 'William's Hill'; the grassy mound 500 yards to the south-west of where the present castle stands. These earthworks mark the site of a wooden motte and bailey castle built by Alan Rufus or 'Alan the Red', nephew of William the Conqueror, on land granted in 1069 by his victorious uncle. This first fortification at Middleham was intended to guard access to Coverdale and to protect the road from Richmond to Skipton, though by the end of the twelfth century the earlier fortification was abandoned in favour of the present one begun in 1190, centered around the massive stone keep of three storied, twelve foot thick walls and still an imposing structure in spite of its ruinous state.

There are also some local legends of a supernatural nature attached to William's Hill, namely the sounds of battle heard in the vicinity of the mound, accompanied by a ghostly charging knight on horseback thundering down toward the castle ruins, possibly drowning out the strains of ghostly muffled music also heard in the environs of Middleham Castle.

Willance's Leap, Whitecliffe Scar, near Richmond

A mile or so upstream from Richmond is Whitecliffe Scar, looking south over the valley of Swaledale, and where there are not one but three commemorations in stone to the man who survived a 200 foot drop here in November 1606.

Robert Willance was a prosperous tradesman in Richmond who enjoyed riding out alone up dale, whatever the weather. On an obviously inclement November day in 1606, approaching Deepdale, Willance and his mount were enveloped in thick mist, and in the severely restricted visibility ended

Boar or Bear? Difficult to discern as this now lumpen creature has been weathered beyond all recognition...

Robert Willance's grave in the churchyard of St Mary's, Richmond – in accordance with his wishes, his amputated leg buried ten years previously was exhumed and re-interred with the rest of his mortal remains

up making an unplanned leap over the edge of Whitecliffe Scar. While his horse was killed instantly, Willance miraculously escaped the fall with a broken leg. To give thanks for his escape Willance erected an inscribed stone at the place of his unintended leap, replaced in 1734, and again in 1815 and then again in 1843. In 1906 an obelisk was erected commemorating the tercentenary of the 'Leap', and in 2006 a third stone was set up to mark the 400th anniversary of the much remembered event.

In a final aside to this incredible tale, as a result of his fall, Willance's broken leg was necessarily amputated, and given separate burial in the churchyard of St Mary's in Richmond. A decade later, before his death Willance had expressed in his will a strong desire to be reunited with his amputated limb after he died. His wishes respected, the leg was duly exhumed and reunited with the remainder of Willance's body, and buried in its 'second' grave on 12th February 1616.

Wishing Tree, Flintergill, Dentdale

Certainly a tree worth visiting, as it is said that this Oak will make your wishes come true! It used to be believed that divine spirits lived in trees, ancient and wise, offering healing magic, wisdom and insight, with the tradition of 'wish trees' dating back hundreds if not thousands of years.

At Flintergill, where a natural arch has been created by the exposed and expansive root system of the tree, it is said that if you walk underneath the roots and around the tree three times 'deosil', that is to say in the direction of the sun, then your wish will be granted.

Close by are the curiously named 'Dancing Flags' – an expansive of flat stones at the water's edge where washerwomen are reputed to have 'danced' up and down on clothes to get them clean. In deference to this tale, in 2002 traditional clog dancers performed the 'Flintergill Jig' on this stretch of exposed riverbed, though in this instance no dirty clothing was involved!

Witch of the Woods House, Azerley, near Ripon

The eerily named Witch of the Woods House is located in an isolated spot surrounded by trees on three sides, and though now partially restored, it is easy to imagine cobwebs stretched over the once paneless windows and bats roosting in the eaves giving rise to the name. Only accessible by fording a stream called Kex Beck, the Witch of the Woods House was set with a datestone inscribed:

'W' (George Wells)
G M
1717

Possibly referring to the younger son of the Wells family of nearby Cowmyers Farm, George Wells was probably bequeathed the property or made alterations to it in that year. A further later reference to the house comes from the Kirkby Malzeard Parish Records, that in 1844 the body of one Thomas Dallow was conveyed in the Parish Hearse from 'Witch-in-the-Wood House' to Azerley along the private road with the owner's permission.

Whether or not a witch has ever inhabited the woods surrounding the house, it currently stands empty... and perhaps understandably so!

The isolated Witch of the Woods House

X

'X' Marks The Spot

The beloved trope of Robert Louis Stevenson's 'Treasure Island' can surely be applied to a treasure map of the Yorkshire Dales, as here we have buried riches aplenty...

At Middleham Castle, the now extensive roofless ruin that was once the fortified royal palace and childhood home to Richard III, it is intriguingly rumoured that a hoard of treasure is buried somewhere in the castle environs. It is said that if you run around the castle three times, where you stop the treasure will be found, sadly though nobody thought to recorded a starting point for this race to riches and so the treasure and the tale remain intact.

More buried treasure is waiting to be found within the ruined walls of Bowes Castle, situated on the old Roman road running through Stainmore and leading on to Cataractonium, or Catterick as we now know it today. Bowes Castle was constructed on the foundations of the Roman fort Lavatrae, built in the late first century, traces of the garrison that once protected the Roman road on its course across the north Pennines, the modern route now followed by the busy A66, still visible in the fields south of St Giles Church. During the final days of the waning Roman occupation and a general disintegration in discipline, the soldiers stationed at Lavatrae went on a plundering spree of the surrounding villages, laying their hands on anything of value, especially gold... Eventually the victimised local inhabitants banded together in numbers strong enough to storm the fort in a revenge attack and massacred the Roman soldiers to a man. However, clearly suspecting a local backlash the soldiers had already secretly buried all the ill-gotten loot, but with the entire garrison annihilated the hidden location remained a mystery.

It is said though, that on the anniversary of the massacre the ghosts of the murdered soldiers appear at Bowes Castle to re-enact the burying of the treasure, and associated folklore dating to the sixteenth century tells of two local men who had the splendid idea of hiding in the ruins on the anniversary so that they might observe the ghostly legionaries and ascertain exactly where to dig. The enterprising pair were rewarded with the vision of a procession of phantom Roman soldiers carrying a huge chest of gold, they making careful note of where this was buried. However, before either had the opportunity to retrieve the treasure, both men met a violent death within hours of each other...

The first was murdered by his greedy associate, who on proceeding to scrabble in the dirt at the appropriate spot was beckoned by a mysterious bloody red hand and dragged by forces unseen over the fields to the banks of the River Greta where his body was discovered the next day. Understandably for many years Lavatrae was shunned as a dark and sinister place, especially around the anniversary of the bloodbath that had taken place so many centuries before.

The ruins of Bowes Castle, built on the foundations of the Roman fort Lavatrae

At Pendragon Castle near the hamlet of Outhgill in remote Mallerstang Dale, the alleged strong-hold of Uther Pendragon – see his entry under the letter 'U' for more of the legendary father of King Arthur – a treasure protecting phantom black hen is said to inhabit the environs of the castle ruins, deterring any would-be treasure hunters from digging for the booty supposedly buried therein. This inexhaustible chicken will eternally replace any freshly dug soil as quickly as it can be excavated!

The atmospheric remains of Pendragon Castle, near Outhgill

Though the Pendragon phantom chicken may seem an unusual guardian, there is a strong tradition of hidden treasure being safeguarded by feathered custodians, with hens, cockerels, ravens and eagles (some even consuming the odd foolhardy treasure hunter) standing guard, and another tale of a sentinel rooster can be found in William Henderson's *Notes on the folk-lore of the northern counties of England and the borders* (1879). Relating to a hoard of buried gold in Swaledale, possibly hidden by retreating Celtic tribesmen who were renowned for their fine gold jewellery, Henderson wrote that he had learnt *'from Mr. Robinson, of Hill House, Reeth, Yorkshire, that in his neighbourhood as in many others is a place called Maiden's Castle, in which tradition avers a chest of gold is buried. "Many attempts," he says, "have been made to gain possession of the treasure, and one party of adventurers actually came up to the chest and laid hold of it, when a hen appeared, flapped her wings, and put out the light. This occurred three times, and the men were obliged to desist. The next day was Sunday, still they returned to the place. A violent storm of thunder and rain came on, however, and the 'drift,' in miners' phrase, 'ran'. My informant, an old man of the place, knew this, he said, for a fact.'*

Yet another hen is involved with the legend of the giant's treasure concealed beneath Stony Raise Cairn, the round barrow to the south of Addleborough Hill near Bainbridge in Wensleydale, and the obstacle which caused the giant to trip and lose his grip and drop his precious load. It is said that to this day that the treasure remains beneath the cairn and bizarrely can only be uncovered with the assistance of a hen and an ape! Why an ape should be involved remains unexplained, but needless to say this theory has yet to be put to the test.

The treasure hidden within Dob Park Lodge, an early seventeenth century hunting lodge overlooking the Washburn Valley, may be difficult to locate as the original directions to this hoard reference some internal features, and as Dob Park is now a ruined shell (the lodge's state of collapse already well advanced when Turner painted his *On the Washburn, under Folly Hall* in 1815) the clues may well prove useless. There is a further impediment in the shape of the huge saucer eyed black dog (perhaps a cousin of the Barguests mentioned under the letter 'B') that is said to watch over the hidden treasure within the lodge, and unusually also possessing the power of speech! In the late 1800s, a foolhardy, and it must be said very drunk individual ventured to explore the vaults of the dilapidated building, the entrance to which was supposedly at the foot of a once winding stairway. Claiming that he actually saw a great chest of gold, presumably he was too inebriated to follow-up on his discovery, and one must assume that the gold and the conversational canine remain in the ruined lodge to this day…

Y

Yan, Tan, Tether, Mether...
This age old method of sheep counting is believed to be Celtic in origin, and the use of this traditional numbering system was common among shepherds, especially in the Dales. To assist the necessary and frequent head-counts of their flocks, the following is recited:

> "*Yan, tan, tether, mether, pimp*
> *Sether, hether, hother, dother, dick*
> *Yan dick, tan dick, tether dick, mether dick, bumfit*
> *Yan bumfit, tan bumfit, tether bumfit, mether bumfit, gigot*"

Yan!

'Yan' obviously 'one', the rhyme numerically rising to 'gigot' when the number of sheep reached twenty. As Celtic numbering systems tend to be vigesimal, that is based on the number twenty, to count a large number of sheep a shepherd would repeatedly count to 'gigot' then place a mark on the ground, or move his hand to another notch on his crook, or drop a pebble into his pocket to represent each score – certainly putting a new slant on the mental exercise of 'counting sheep' to lull yourself to sleep at night!

Ye Olde Naked Man, Settle
Facing on to Settle's busy market square is the 'Naked Man' of Settle, a figurative datestone set above the the door of 'Ye Olde Naked Man' cafe, once an inn of the same name. It is said that when Queen Victoria visited the town the naked man was covered lest he offend the prudish monarch, but in spite of this interim obscurity he has surveyed Settle since 1663, the date inscribed on the date plaque he holds to cover his modesty. In actual fact, the naked man is clothed as on closer examination the buttons of his jacket and the

The 'naked' man himself

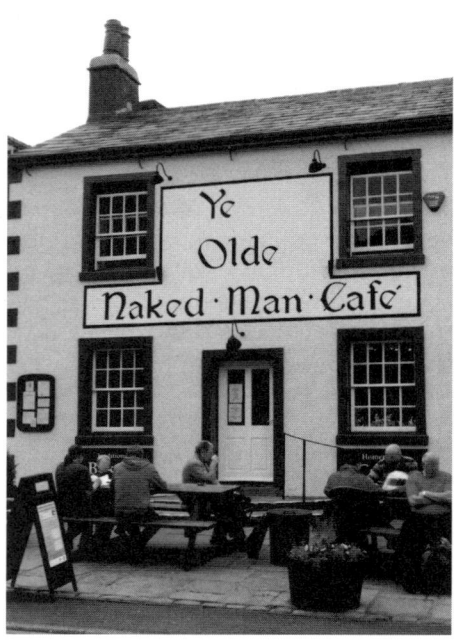

'Ye Olde Naked Man' Cafe facing on to Settle's market square

bottom of his breeches can be discerned. Naked or not, he is in good company as less than a mile from Settle, in the village of Langcliffe there is a 'naked lady' depicted on a datestone of 1660, her modesty covered by the initials 'LSMS' referring to Lawrence and Margaret Swainson, presumably the owners of the former inn bearing the datestone and closed in 1862. Though this naked lady appears to have a hint of a beard, she still has a smile on her face!

Yordas' Cave, Kingsdale, near Ingleton

This former Victorian 'show cave' found in Yordas' Wood in Kingsdale near Ingleton was the reputed lair of the infant-devouring Norse giant Yordas.

If exploring this wonderful place a torch is a must to fully appreciate the large main chamber – the 'Great Hall of the Giant Yordas' and the underground waterfall chamber at the back of the cave. In 1892 Harry Speight described the natural wonders of this limestone cave as "*...the dead, old genius of the cave – grim Yordas in his coat of mail, with mighty frozen arm and clenched fist, raised in seeming defiance of anyone who dared to dispute his sovereignty of these priceless, gem-studded halls*".

Presumably by the time Charlotte Brontë visited the cave the giant had retreated back into Norse myth, as it is believed that here she found the inspiration for the 'Fairy Cave' mentioned in her novel *Jane Eyre*, the character of Mr Rochester regaling his young ward, Adele as follows:

"*It was a fairy, and come from Elf-land, it said; and its errand was to make me happy: I must go with it out of the common world to a lonely place – such as the moon, for instance – and it nodded its head towards her horn, rising over Hay-hill: it told me of the alabaster cave and silver vale where we might live. I said I should like to go; but reminded it, as you did me, that I had no wings to fly.*"

The foreboding dark entrance to Yordas Cave, somewhat hidden by the flourishing hawthorn trees of early summer – the author was unable to discern the presence of any fairies!

No wings are necessary when visiting the cave today, just fresh batteries in your torch!

Yore Mill, Aysgarth Falls, Wensleydale

This former water mill located on the River Ure at Aysgarth Falls is picturesquely set against one of Wensleydales's most famous beauty spots, where the waters tumbling over a series of broad limestone steps form the upper, middle and lower falls drawing thousands of visitors each year to the Aysgarth Falls National Park Centre.

Built in 1784 by Birkbecks of Settle, the four storey Grade II listed former cotton mill is one of the earliest examples of an 'industrial-ised' mill outside of an urban

Yore Mill, Aysgarth Falls - Yorkshire's unlikely connection to Garibaldi's Italian Redcoats

setting. However, after a fire destroyed the interior in 1852 production turned to worsted which was given out to knitters in the dale to make into stockings and jerseys. But with the advent of machine made goods, Yore Mill was left with over seven thousand jerseys on their hands, and these eventually ended up being dyed red and sent to Italy as uniforms for General Garibaldi's Redcoats to wear in the fight for a united Italy.

Yorke's Folly, near Pateley Bridge
Visible from Pateley Bridge, this Nidderdale landmark is a fake ruin, the original folly comprising of three columns, known as 'The Three Stoups', though today only the two impressive towers that once supported an arch still stand, the third column blown down in a severe storm in 1893.

It is likely that the folly was constructed as part of the landscaping of the area when the Yorke family built their new hall at Bewerley in 1815-20. In a philanthropic gesture, John Yorke employed local labour as economically the district was hard hit by the Napoleonic Wars, thus saving many from poverty. As a result he was known as 'the poor man's friend'.

Using local gritstone with ashlar facings, it is thought John Yorke had in mind the ruins of Fountains Abbey when designing the folly, lay brothers from Fountains having built the original Bewerley Hall.

A few hundred yards from Yorke's Folly on the slope at the north-western end of Guise Cliffe is another curiosity in the guise of the 'Crocodile Rock', a Gritstone outcrop fancifully named as the rocks resembles the gaping jaws of the snappy reptile, yet the expansive views out across Nidderdale through it's open mouth are quite breathtaking.

Z

Zetland Street, Northallerton

Remembered in one of the street names of the county town of North Yorkshire, Zetland Street in Northallerton was named for the Earl of Zetland.

By the close of the seventeenth century, if not earlier, Northallerton had become the administrative centre for the North Riding, and this is a position it has retained. The Registry for Deeds for the North Riding was built and established here in 1736, and the registry and court-house, built in 1782, stand in what is now Zetland Street. Formerly known as the 'back lane' of the town, the street was renamed so that these prestigious edifices could enjoy a rather more illustrious address; there is a Blue Plaque in Zetland Street which reads 'The North Riding Registry of Deeds was built here in 1736. It was converted into a house for the Registrar in 1782'.

Zetland Street's Blue Plaque marking the former site of the North Riding Registry of Deeds, later converted into a house for the Registrar; today 'Register House' is an art gallery

With regard to the Zetland title, this was chosen by Lawrence, 2nd Lord Dundas who was the grandson of Sir Lawrence Dundas Baronet who in 1763 had purchased the Aske Estate, including the imposing Aske Hall, a Georgian country house with parkland attributed to Capability Brown about a mile and a half north of Richmond. In return for providing financial assistance to the Duke and Duchess of Kent, the future Queen Victoria's parents, the 2nd Lord Dundas was created the 1st Earl of Zetland in 1838 on the day of the young queen's coronation. Among the many estates bought by his grandfather was one on Zetland (which is now better known as Shetland) thus, when Lawrence was promoted to the earldom, he chose Zetland for his new title.

Zion in the Dales?!

Jerusalem in North Yorkshire I hear you ask? Surely a great geographical blunder! Not quite... While Zion is a place name often used as a synonym for Jerusalem and commonly referring to Mount Zion, the hill just outside the walls of the Holy City, in the Dales there are, though few and far between 'Zion' chapels harking back to the days of Methodist zeal.

The movement deriving its inspiration from the life and teachings of John Wesley, of the non-conformist groups emerging from the established church in the eighteenth century, Methodism in particular had a big following in these parts. Wesley preached regularly in Yorkshire on his evangelistic travels, first visiting Swaledale in 1761, and of the Wesleyan chapels that emerged, and still a common feature of many Dales towns and villages today, a few examples of Zion remain, namely the Mount Zion Chapel at Garsdale Head.

The Mount Zion Chapel at Garsdale Head, a Primitive Methodist meeting-place which is still used for special events

Located at a bleak spot overlooking the head of Garsdale, the village of Garsdale Station has no real centre, just a scattered community with a line of former railway staff cottages, a number of isolated farms, the Moorcock Inn and the Mount Zion Chapel.

A familiar roadside landmark as one passes under the Dandymire Viaduct and over the county line from the Dales into Cumbria, the Mount Zion Chapel was opened in 1876, the same year that passenger traffic began on the nearby Settle to Carlisle Railway, and served a local community of railway employees and farmers. Matching the building style of the railway workers cottages (the chapel was built by the Midland Railway contractors), occasional services are still held here, and with its railway connections and historic interest, the Garsdale Mount Zion Chapel remains one of the most beautiful and best decorated of all wayside Wesleyan chapels.